AMERICA

The USA

TIME-LIFE BOOKS/AMSTERDAM

COOKERY AROUND THE WORLD

AMERICA: The USA

ANGELA G. GRANT

Recipe photographs: Foodphotography Eising

I	The Northeast
1	Vermont
2	New Hampshire
3	Massachusetts
4	Connecticut
5	Rhode Island
6	New Jersey
7	Delaware
8	Maryland
II	The South
III	Louisiana
IV	The Midwest
V	The Great Plains & The Rocky Mountains
VI	The Southwest
VII	The West Coast
VIII	Alaska & Hawaii

CONTENTS

AMERICA: THE USA– LAND OF PLENTY

One trip to America can do no more than reveal a few of the countless aspects of this vast and multifaceted land, which is hardly surprising when one considers that the United States is roughly the size of Europe, or that the United Kingdom is smaller than the state of Wyoming and France would fit very comfortably into Texas. But one can always look forward to the next time. From New England's picturesque bays and fishing villages to the Great Plains' grain fields and prairies, from Alaska's glaciers to the sunny West Coast, from the Southwest's deserts and canyons to the Louisiana bayous, each region has its own special appeal.

In the east, between the Appalachian Mountains and the coast, the Atlantic metropolitan belt includes the great cities of Washington, Boston and New York, the frenetic, vibrant "Big Apple". In the west, which lures visitors with the promise of beach life, fun and Hollywood glamour, are Los Angeles and one of the nation's most beautiful cities, San Francisco. Between them lie the Great Plains and the Rockies, where the Apache, Sioux and Cherokee once hunted bison on the open prairies, and the haunting, sacred places of the native Americans still inspire awe.

Another kind of magic can be found in the Southern states where, on the slow-moving Mississippi, paddle steamers still operate for the tourists. Stately plantation mansions lying hidden at the end of long, tree-lined avenues evoke visions of former splendours, when cotton was "king".

America is also a land of national parks, wilderness areas and wildlife reserves, and all 50 states have their own state parks. Large areas remain unspoiled and, from the Arctic north to the subtropical south, the flora and fauna match the wide diversity of the country's climate and terrain.

No matter where you go, America is a great place. The spontaneous, unassuming friendliness of the people, the many wonders of nature, the dynamic towns and cities, offer something for everyone. And the country also finds a way to visitors' hearts through their stomachs. The USA is the world's leading agricultural nation and nowhere is food more plentiful or the choice more varied.

Whether it is fast food such as charcoal-grilled hamburgers and French fries or baked potatoes with soured cream topping, or traditional dishes such as clam chowder, Brunswick stew, blueberry muffins or pecan pie, American cuisine has a wonderful selection of foods on offer. These have evolved over the centuries through the input of many immigrant cultures and cuisines. In restaurants and diners, the service is efficient and enthusiastic, and portions are truly enormous.

American vineyards produce some excellent wines. The best known of these come from California and the Northwest, but there are also many vineyards in the east and south.

The first chapter of this book invites you on a journey through the United States, introducing the country, its people, and the culinary preferences and specialities of the various regions. Starting with breakfasts and brunches, the recipe chapters are then arranged in the traditional order of the menu. Only authentic recipes are included and step-by-step instructions are given for each one. There are suggestions for variations and drinks, plus information about specific local products.

Finally, there are menu suggestions to help you plan American meals for different occasions and seasons, and a glossary of less familiar ingredients, culinary words or expressions.

A MELTING POT OF CULTURES

The roots of American cuisine go back to the original inhabitants. The native Americans hunted bison and game birds such as wild turkeys. They caught fish in abundance from the sea and rivers, used honey and maple syrup for sweetening and gathered wild plants and berries. Some also grew maize and beans.

The first settlers grew their own vegetables and fruits from seeds brought with them but, with the help of the natives, they also learnt to adapt traditional recipes to the local food resources—for example, before wheat was widely grown, maize became the main staple and cornmeal replaced wheat flour. Spoonbread, muffins, cakes and puddings made of cornmeal are still widely eaten today.

From the 17th century on, America became a haven for the world's oppressed. English, French, Germans, Dutch, Scandinavians, Irish, Chinese, Poles, Russians, Italians and others such as Puerto Ricans and Mexicans, came to America in order to flee from poverty, or religious or political persecution in their home country.

As new waves of immigrants arrived from all over the world, they brought with them their customs, traditions and recipes. These widely differing cultures have all helped to create the American cuisine of today.

Americans are proud of their origins and the traditions of their forebears. Despite today's massive distribution and transportation networks, fast foods and supermarkets, variations in regional cooking—depending on which ethnic groups predominate—continue.

For example, English influences have remained strongest in New England and the northeast; German cooking still prevails in parts of the Midwest and Pennsylvania (the Pennsylvania Dutch were German, not Dutch). In the Southwest, the cuisine is largely Spanish and Mexican, and the steaks and chili con carne served from chuck wagons to the cowboys on the open prairie are universally popular.

The Africans, first brought as slaves to the South in the 17th century, have left their mark on Southern cuisine. Mingled with the French and Spanish, their style of cooking produced the spicy Cajun and Creole cuisines for which Louisiana is renowned.

Americans love to gather for an open-air barbecue or picnic. In summer the weather is good enough anywhere in the country. Open hospitality and a congenial atmosphere are the order of the day and, since these events tend to be organized on every conceivable occasion, it is not unusual to receive an invitation on the spur of the moment. Such an invitation should be accepted in the spirit in which it was offered—and you won't regret it.

Fish abound in the northeast coastal waters and angling is a popular pastime.

American football is a major national sport. Below, Harvard plays a team from Princeton in a university match in Boston.

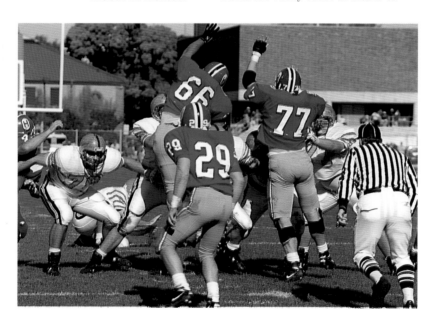

The Northeast

New England

Ask any American, and he or she will urge you to go to New England in the fall when, between September and November, the leaves turn to dazzling yellows, brilliant oranges and flaming reds. Ablaze with colour in the warm autumn sun, the woods are an unforgettable sight as they stand out against the intense blue of the sky.

But every season has its delights and the region, with its huge forests, clear lakes, mountains and extensive coastline, is a popular destination for nature-lovers. Inland the terrain in summer is ideal for hiking or camping, boating or canoeing, and freshwater fishing. The winters are cold but there is excellent skiing in Vermont and New Hampshire's White Mountains. In spring, all over Maine and Vermont the maple trees are tapped to obtain America's favourite syrup, first used as a sweetener by the Indians.

From the rocky coast of Maine to Rhode Island and Connecticut, five of the six states border the Atlantic. The Gulf Stream keeps ocean temperatures above 20°C in summer, making bathing from the many beaches very pleasant and sailing a major sport. From sheltered harbours along this coast 18th and 19th-century fishing fleets set sail to catch cod and to harpoon whales; (the now-protected whales can still be spotted off Cape Cod.)

The region's most important city is 360-year-old Boston, cradle of American Independence. A walk through the narrow, winding streets of the old town, following the "Freedom Trail" (marked by a red line), takes one past many historic landmarks. The city is home to the Boston Symphony Orchestra and is also a major centre of learning—boasting both Harvard University and the Massachusetts Institute of Technology.

Many of the earliest European settlers came to Massachusetts and some of the coastal towns are part of an historic preservation area. It was here that, in 1620, the Pilgrim Fathers arrived in the *Mayflower*. Their early efforts at crop-growing failed and had it not been for the friendly Algonquin Indians they might not have survived their first year. The Algonquin taught them to hunt wild turkeys, pick berries in the woodlands and catch all manner of fish and shellfish, as well as how to cultivate the native staple foods: maize, beans and pumpkins.

As a mark of gratitude, the settlers invited the Indians to a sumptuous feast. A stuffed turkey was served at this first Thanksgiving meal, and ever since then, throughout the USA, no Thanksgiving dinner is complete without turkey. Among other recipes learnt from the Indians is *succotash*, sweetcorn and beans cooked together.

Subsequent settlers grew apples and pears, root vegetables, cabbages, onions and cereals and adapted their homeland recipes to suit their new life. Short growing seasons meant produce was often dried, smoked, preserved or salted. Warm, satisfying winter dishes such as New England boiled dinner and Boston baked beans are still popular today. But New England is best known for its delicious seafood, especially lobsters and other shellfish.

Middle Atlantic States

New York State, Pennsylvania, New Jersey, Maryland and Delaware are steeped in United States history: many major events in the American War of Independence and the American Civil War took place in this region.

The coast, with its numerous seaside resorts, belongs almost entirely to New Jersey. A little further inland, a chain of cities runs from Washington DC, capital of the United States and seat of federal government, up to New England. With New York city as its focal point, this urban stretch of commercial and industrial centres is sometimes referred to as the Atlantic metropolitan belt. To the west, the Appalachian Mountains extend across Pennsylvania, New Jersey and New York State towards Lakes Ontario and Erie.

The climate is milder than in New England and the land more fertile. Apples are grown in profusion and used to make, for example, deliciously sweet applesauce cake or *schnitz un knepp*, a dish of ham, apples and dumplings, brought to Pennsylvania by German

settlers. The Dutch, who colonized New Jersey from 1655, introduced waffles, pancakes and cookies. Farmers from many different religious communities settled in Pennsylvania, among them the Amish, a sect who shunned modern innovations and today still live much as they did at the turn of the century.

In stark contrast, the pulsating skyscraper metropolis of New York City is a cosmopolitan mecca for Americans and foreigners alike. Many immigrant communities settled here with their diverse cultures, religions, lifestyles and their own food specialities—such as spicy beef pastrami and bagels (ring-shaped bread rolls), introduced by Jewish immigrants. New York's own Waldorf salad was created in the eponymous luxury hotel.

Bright autumn sun highlights this Vermont farmhouse nestling among the trees. The flaming reds, oranges and gold of New England's woodlands in the fall are a major tourist attraction.

Once killed for their delicate meat, which tastes like a cross between fish and chicken, Florida's wild alligators are now a protected species.

An old-world paddle steamer takes visitors at Walt Disney World in Florida on a journey back to Colonial days. The Disney theme parks are a fantasy experience for children and adults alike.

The South and Florida

The South

A haunting blues echoing from a smoky bar in Memphis, gospel singing in a little church in Georgia or bouncy Dixieland jazz in an Alabama saloon: to many people this is what "The South" conjures up. For others, the names of Virginia, Carolina, Kentucky, Georgia, Mississippi, Tennessee and Alabama bring to mind images of Scarlett O'Hara, Rhett Butler and the classic Hollywood movie, *Gone with the Wind*.

The hot, often sultry climate of much of the region is reflected in the general lifestyle. The hectic pace typical of the big cities in the northeast is missing in the South; Southerners like to take things a little easier. Areas such as the southeast have especially hot and humid summers, and holidaymakers often prefer the slightly cooler spring and autumn for swimming or boating, tennis or golf, or visiting historic sites.

Here are towns such as Georgia's modern capital, Atlanta, birthplace of Martin Luther King, and Charleston, the handsome, aristocratic port of South Carolina with its public parks and many 18th and 19th-century buildings. Shaded by great trees, most of the majestic former summer residences of the rich plantation and slave owners sport classical columned porticos.

For those who prefer summer spas or winter skiing, there are the mountains of West Virginia and Virginia—Thomas Jefferson's home state. The Mississippi Valley states of Tennessee, Kentucky and Arkansas, land of cotton and tobacco, also boast some of the USA's most beautiful mountain scenery. Blues, Dixieland, rock'n'roll, soul and country music all have their roots here—celebrated annually with such festivals as Nashville's International Country Music Fair. In August, Elvis Presley fans flock to Memphis to commemorate the anniversary of his death.

Tobacco was the major crop in the South in the 18th century. With the invention of the cotton gin in 1793 and the growth of textile industries, cotton became the basis of Southern economy. After the Civil War—when over 600,000 Americans lost their lives and the South lost much of its wealth and splendour—the end of slavery resulted in the break-up of many large plantations into smallholdings, often owned by ex-slaves. But not until the beginning of this century did cotton-growing decline. Even today, although major crops include rice, sorghum, peanuts, soybeans, maize and tobacco, US cotton comprises nearly a third of the world's total cotton exports.

Southerners are proud of their cooking traditions, which incorporate both old-style plantation cuisine and the simple, filling food eaten by the

slaves and known as "soul food". Hot cornbread, Southern fried chicken, Hoppin' John (black-eyed peas and rice) and pecan pie are served in restaurants everywhere. Along the Atlantic coast and Gulf of Mexico, fish, prawns, oysters and crabs are among the region's main produce.

Mild winters in the more southerly states are suitable for growing tropical fruit. Further north, Virginia and the Carolinas are renowned for bacon and Smithfield Ham. Georgia grows peaches and peanuts, while rice flourishes in North and South Carolina as well as in the Mississippi Valley.

Florida

The holiday state of Florida, where the Spaniards established the first European settlement in America in 1565, boasts a wealth of plant and animal life. Once covered by forests, some have made way for plantations of citrus fruits and sugar cane, grazing for cattle, and for cities such as Miami,

with its population of nearly 2 million, over half of Hispanic origin.

The remaining forests, nature parks, lakes and springs are popular outdoor holiday destinations for hiking, camping, picnicking or shooting the rapids in canoes. Along the coast, there are endless beaches and resorts with restaurants and nightclubs, golf courses and yacht harbours. At the tip of the peninsula are the Everglades, the country's biggest subtropical national park with mangrove swamps and grass marshes. Florida Keys, a string of 31 tropical islands at the most southerly point of the USA, can be reached from the mainland by a series of interconnecting bridges.

Apart from citrus fruits, from which are made delicious desserts such as Key lime pie, local specialities include fish and shellfish such as pompano, red snapper, shark and spiny lobsters. Wild alligators are a protected species, but alligator farms ensure that grilled alligator steaks are still on the menu.

Miami's numerous flamboyant cars rival those of most American cities.

Cartoon characters such as Donald Duck (below) appear in many guises at Disney World.

Louisiana

Although one of the Mississippi Valley states, Louisiana has a rather different history from the rest of the American South. The majority of its population is of Catholic French or Spanish and African origin, and its Creole and Cajun cooking is renowned worldwide.

The first Europeans to arrive here were Spanish explorers in the early 16th century. But it was not until the end of the 17th century, when France claimed all the lands drained by the Mississippi River and its tributaries for Louis XIV, naming it Louisiana, that colonies were established.

In the following century the land west of the Mississippi transferred to Spain, but was regained by Napoleon in 1800. Three years later, President Thomas Jefferson negotiated to buy it from France for $15 million. At a stroke, this doubled the territory held by the United States and secured access to the Gulf of Mexico. Both the land (of which the present state is the southernmost part) and transaction became known as the Louisiana Purchase.

Louisiana is a region of lakes and rivers, ideal for fishing and outdoor activities. In the north, the hills are covered with pine forests, while bordering the Gulf of Mexico are the Louisiana bayous—a series of silent, sluggish rivers, overhung by moss-draped oaks and strange vegetation, winding their way through farmlands, swamps and marshes.

West of New Orleans is the traditional home of the Cajuns, or Acadians, the descendants of French people who found their way here in the mid-18th century, after the English persecuted their colony in eastern Canada and deported them. The Cajuns developed their own unique style of cooking and music, and spoke their own dialect of French.

Along the Mississippi River between Baton Rouge, Louisiana's capital, and New Orleans many of the pre-Civil War mansions on the old sugar and cotton plantations have been restored and are a popular tourist attraction.

Few can resist the fascination of lively New Orleans, birthplace of Louis "Satchmo" Armstrong and stronghold of jazz. Many distinguished writers have lived here for a time, including William Faulkner and Tennessee Williams. The old French quarter—or Vieux Carré—with its handsome houses, colourful shops and boutiques, art galleries and Creole restaurants,

There is a fascinating beauty about the strangely silent vegetation bordering the sluggish rivers and streams of southern Louisiana's bayou country.

has a special kind of magic. This is the heart of the city's jazz. The infectious sound of a trumpet or saxophone can be heard on every corner, and street musicians play daily in Jackson Square. Every evening jazz rings out from the bars on Bourbon Street.

The New Orleans Carnival, before Lent, is a crowded, boisterous and colourful affair. On Shrove Tuesday, *Mardi Gras*, everyone dances through the streets in extravagant costumes and partying goes on until morning. An unmissable gastronomic event is the June Food Festival, where one can see at first hand how New Orleans' chefs create the Cajun and Creole dishes for which the city is justly famous.

It is said that, in Louisiana, Creole is the cooking of the city while Cajun belongs to the country. Both have their origins in French cuisine adapted to the foods available in the New World and inheriting many characteristics

from slave food. Raw ingredients are much the same, with rice as a staple. Crabs and freshwater crayfish are particular specialities; vegetables include yams, aubergines and tropical squash called mirlitons.

There are Creole and Cajun versions of, for example, gumbo (seafood or meat soup thickened with okra) and jambalaya (Louisiana's answer to the Spanish *paella*). But Creole dishes, once the food of French and Spanish aristocrats, with their subtle sauces and discreet use of herbs such as thyme and bay leaves, have more affinity to *grande cuisine*. The more robust country fare of the Cajuns reflects a less affluent, more strenuous history. Dishes are highly-seasoned with herbs, spices and chili peppers, and served in generous quantities with vegetables. A little Tabasco sauce—made here—is essential in chilled avocado soup and seafood gumbo.

Street musicians jazz it up for passers-by in lively New Orleans. Strategically situated on the Mississippi River, New Orleans is Louisiana's largest and most important city.

Viewed from the roof of the YMCA in the fading evening light, Chicago's skyscraper skyline has a magical quality.

The Midwest and Great Lakes

The Midwest

A region of gently rolling hills, huge river valleys, woods and farmlands, the Midwest also boasts four of the five Great Lakes and the USA's third-largest city, Chicago. Other important cities include Cincinnati, Cleveland, Detroit and Indianapolis.

Since the 18th century, waves of immigrants from many nationalities and cultures have arrived here to farm and mine, work in factories, steel and timber mills, or build railways. Germans, Poles, Italians, French, Irish, Scandinavians and others have left their mark on both the region's lifestyle and cooking.

One example of how European dishes were adopted in the New World is the pasty. Introduced to Michigan by Cornish miners in the mid-19th century, the pasty became so popular that every community in the state, whether Swedish, Finnish, Polish or Italian, soon had its own version.

Today, Chicago and cities such as Milwaukee still have many ethnic communities with their own traditions, shops and restaurants, where English may be the second language.

The great industrial and art metropolis of Chicago has been a major trading centre for cattle and farm produce since the arrival of the train made it the USA's most important rail junction—America's first steak houses opened here as a result of the huge trade in beef. Much sightseeing can be done on foot. After the great fire of 1871, most of the city had to be rebuilt and many of the handsome skyscrapers, museums and other

Hamburgers, the world's favourite American food, originated here, as did hot dogs—both were first sold at the 1904 World Fair in St. Louis.

The Great Lakes

Although some landscape around Lake Michigan is marred by heavy industry, there is also beautiful lakeside scenery, a rugged coastline that can be explored by boat, beaches with enormous sand dunes, little resort towns and cherry orchards. Woodlands in the surrounding countryside are full of game and edible mushrooms.

Round the other four Great Lakes, which are partly in Canada, is a gigantic leisure paradise of parklands and forests where visitors may come across bears, elks and wolves. There are scenic lakeshore drives and ample opportunities for swimming, fishing and water sports. Perch, salmon, sturgeon and pike are caught in these waters and sold fresh or smoked.

At the western end of Lake Superior, in a protected, densely forested area, there are more than 1,000 lakes where canoeing is now a major sport.

South of Lake Erie, spanning Ohio, Pennsylvania and New York State, is eastern USA's biggest grape-growing district. Most of the wine here is made from Concord grapes, developed from hardy native American *Vitis labrusca*.

When visiting Lake Erie, a trip to Niagara Falls in New York State should not be missed. Despite the crowds, watching the 300-metre-wide American Falls crashing down 50 metres or so is an unforgettable, if deafening, experience. The Horseshoe Falls, on the Canadian side of Goat Island, are just as spectacular.

buildings, including the 442-metre-high Sears Tower, until recently the world's tallest building, are the work of America's most famous architects.

The Midwest's natural resources include fish such as trout, perch and bass from the lakes and rivers, and game. Wild rice, first cultivated by the American Indians of Minnesota, is grown here. There is a thriving cheese industry, begun by Swiss and German immigrants in the last century. The latter also brought with them the secret of brewing beer.

In the west and south of the region, where nomadic native Americans once survived by hunting bison and gathering wild plants, roads stretch across the wide open spaces and gently rolling hills of America's "corn belt". The vast areas of maize also feed the cattle and pigs that provide prime meat.

The awesome, grandiose Niagara Falls, one in Canada the other in New York State, are a favourite destination for honeymooners. The Niagara River and Falls are the drainage outlet for the four upper Great Lakes into Lake Ontario.

Bison, or American buffalo, once freely roamed the prairies. Now the few that remain graze in national parks and nature reserves.

"Steamboat Geyser" spouts boiling water and steam 100 metres into the air. One of Yellowstone National Park's many geysers, it only came to life again in 1978.

The Great Plains and the Rocky Mountains

The Great Plains

From the Dakotas, through Nebraska and Kansas to Oklahoma, the Great Plains are bounded by the mighty peaks of the Rocky Mountains to the west and the Missouri River to the east. Here is where the territory celebrated in books and films as the "Wild West" begins. Reminders are everywhere, from theme parks and Old West towns to museum displays of Indian and pioneer artefacts—even covered-wagon tours along Nebraska's Oregon Trail, complete with cookouts and sleeping under the stars.

The American Indians of the Plains rarely grew crops. They lived off the bison, which in those days moved over the prairies in immense herds. In the 19th century, wagon trains of settlers made their way westwards across this inhospitable land, but the long, cold winters, blizzards, storms and droughts held little appeal for the early farmers. Not until the coming of the railways and the Homestead Act of 1862—which gave anyone prepared to farm for a minimum of five years the right to claim 65 hectares of public land—was there large-scale settlement.

Despite extremes of climate and a hard, sometimes violent life, the Plains farmers turned grasslands into crops, aided by rapidly developing mechanization. Today, large areas of the region—known as the "wheat belt"—are covered in waving fields of grain as far as the eye can see.

To the west, grain and sunflower fields give way to prairies, pine forests and rocky landscapes. The Badlands of South Dakota are a desolate, eroded landscape of pink and rust-coloured gorges, ridges and flat-topped hills. Towering 1,000 metres above the Plains, the Black Hills—now famous for the huge carved heads of four US Presidents on Mount Rushmore—were once the sacred lands of the Sioux Indians, until the discovery of gold and other minerals led the US government to force them onto reservations.

The Rocky Mountains

In an almost unbroken line, the Rocky Mountains stretch from Alaska to the Gulf of Mexico. From the glaciers in Montana to the hot springs of Wyoming and the ski terrain of Colorado, the region known as the Rocky Mountain States is of breathtaking beauty.

The first European settlers were Spanish fur trappers. In the mid-19th century, gold was found in Nevada and Colorado, and prospectors and fortune hunters began to arrive in large numbers. Later, Texan cattle breeders and sheep farmers brought their animals to graze the lower pastures.

Here the "Wild West" is alive and well. At the many rodeos, such as that in June at Reno, Nevada, or the one in the last week of July at Cheyenne, capital of Wyoming, cowboys, who still watch over the herds of cattle, display

daring feats of horsemanship or ride on the backs of untamed bulls.

No visitor should miss Yellowstone National Park, the oldest and best-known of America's many national parks. Covering some 9,000 square kilometres, it is an area of calcareous rock terraces, thermal pools and geysers; forests and waterfalls; and wildlife that includes bison and grizzly bears. The most famous geyser, *Old Faithful*, ejects steaming jets of boiling water high into the air every hour.

With Aspen as its best-known resort, Colorado is the ski capital of America. The Colorado River, which gives the state its name, was so-called by the Spaniards because of the multi-coloured layers of sandstone along its banks. Denver, the capital, once a gold-mining town which achieved importance after it was connected to the railway system in 1870, is today a big commercial and financial centre,

and hub of a major transport network.

Further south, Utah owes much of its fame to the Mormons of Salt Lake City and to its spectacular canyons. One of the most dramatic is Bryce Canyon, a magical landscape of thousands of towering pink, red and purple rock pinnacles rising out of basin-shaped ravines. The formation and erosion of the rocks started 60 million years ago.

The regional cooking is as down-to-earth as the people who settled in the mountains. Beef and lamb are favourites, as are game and wildfowl, and all kinds of berries. Highly seasoned meat loaves are as popular as spare ribs or steaks. Fish from the icy mountain streams are poached in wine or stuffed with fresh herbs. Beans, peaches and melons abound in Colorado, while Mexican influence is strong in all the states bordering the Southwest and many dishes are made with maize, chilies and coriander.

At night, Las Vegas turns into a glittering Eldorado for gamblers from all over the world. Nevada legalized gambling in 1931, but the first luxury casino-hotel in Las Vegas was not built until 1946.

By the light of the setting sun, a group of horses and riders heads towards gigantic rock formations in Monument Valley. The valley, with its huge eroded mesas, soaring buttes and deep canyons, has been home to the Navajo for generations.

The Southwest

Dramatic landscapes of deserts, high plateaus, canyons and rock formations, Navajo and Hopi reservations, cattle ranches, oil wells and large cities such as Dallas all conjure up a larger-than-life image of a region much celebrated in films, books and photography.

The history of the Southwest is closely linked to Spain and Mexico. Conquered by Spaniards in the 16th century, the people came under Mexican rule when that country gained its independence in 1821. Meanwhile, there had been a large influx of farmers and cattle-breeders from America into Texas and, after increasing conflicts between the Mexican rulers and American settlers, the Texans won independence. It joined the Union in 1845, followed soon after by Arizona and New Mexico. The coexistence over

the years of Spaniards and American Indians, Mexicans and Texans, turbulent though it might have been in many respects, left behind a vibrant cultural legacy which is also reflected in the region's cooking.

Since the television series *Dallas*, outsiders see Texas as the state of cattle barons and oil magnates: cowboys, dust and cattle on the one hand, elegance and luxurious living on the other, epitomized by cities such as Dallas and Houston, with their modern architecture and dynamic business life.

But Texas has more to offer; for example, spectacular panoramas can be found in the Big Bend National Park, which takes its name from a huge U-turn in the Rio Grande. Here the immense variety of flora and fauna ranges from Douglas pines to desert cactii and from lynxes and pumas to golden eagles and hummingbirds.

Arizona is a state of vast open spaces where one can travel for hours without ever meeting another human being. All one sees are the plateaux on the horizon, red desert sand and giant cacti in an arid landscape. But when one arrives at, for example, the Grand Canyon everything changes. Despite endless tourists, there are still many peaceful spots where one can stand alone and watch in wonder as the sun rises, casting a spell over the whole valley.

For the most memorable sunsets go to Monument Valley on the Colorado Plateau, where the huge red rock formations, mesas and buttes that dominate the desolate landscape are a favourite location of film makers. Much of the land in this northeastern part of Arizona belongs to the Navajo Nation, and is the largest Indian reservation in America. Near its centre is a Hopi reservation with stone and adobe villages built on high mesas.

Thousand-year-old pictographs on the sheer cliffs of the Canyon de Chelly are a legacy of the ancient Anasazi people who once lived here. Evidence of a much more distant past is found in the Petrified Forest National Park.

Santa Fé, capital of New Mexico, was founded in 1610 by Spanish settlers who built the town on the ruins of a destroyed Indian village at the foot of the Sangre de Cristo Mountains. Today, the architecture bears Indian, Spanish and Anglo-American traces. In this area many American Indian communities live in pueblos and there is a thriving arts and crafts industry. Traces of the 2,000-year-old Pueblo civilization can be seen in the countryside as well as

in the museums. To the north is the village of Taos Pueblo, one of the oldest continuously inhabited communities in the United States.

Over the years, the Southwest has developed one of America's most unusual and interesting culinary styles: Tex-Mex, a mixture of Mexican and Texan cookery. Sweetcorn and beans are typical ingredients, as are chili peppers in all shapes and sizes, and of varying fieriness, which are used not just in the popular chile con carne but in most other dishes as well. Sweetcorn is served as a vegetable; maize is ground into cornmeal and made into cornbread, tortillas and tacos.

Other ingredients in Southwestern cuisine include cumin, pecan nuts and pine-nuts. Near the Gulf of Mexico, the Texan cooking style is more like that of Louisiana and the South, and includes plenty of fish and seafood.

People throughout the region like their food barbecued. When the cowboys drove the great herds of cattle across endless distances, they grilled beef steaks over a huge fire in the open or dug a large pit and roasted a whole steer in it. Today, "cowboy cookouts" are a popular way to entertain. Steaks are still a traditional feature, often served with hashed brown potatoes.

In common with many small towns in America, the main street of Flagstaff, Arizona, is lined with motels competing for customers.

After surviving a major flood, this Texan found an original way of immortalizing his homeland, revealed by a toothy grin.

Charlie Chaplin and Greta Garbo both bathed in the Neptune Pool at Hearst Castle, San Simeon. Once owned by newspaper magnate William Randolph Hearst, the house and grounds attract many visitors.

At the Universal Studios in San Fernando Valley, north of Hollywood, visitors are taken on tours featuring live shows, stunts and special effects.

California and the West Coast

Blessed with a warm, sunny climate and endless beaches for swimming and surfing, Californians appear to lead a relatively carefree existence. There are plenty of opportunities for outdoor sports and outdoor eating, and at night theatres, bars, discos and nightclubs are crowded. But California is a highly productive industrial and agricultural state and Californians work hard to earn their leisure. The region is also an international centre for the arts, film and television, and many writers, artists and musicians have made it their home.

Like the Southwest, the first settlers were Spanish. In the 19th century the wagon trains began to cross the Plains on the Oregon Trail to the West Coast. After Mexican Independence, California became a Mexican province and was ceded to the United States in 1848. That year, gold was discovered and started a gold rush that spread to the rest of the nation, bringing in large numbers of people and creating new towns and cities. The influx of both Americans and immigrants of all nationalities has continued unabated—in 1850, the population of California numbered less than 100,000, today it is over 30 million, making it the most populated state in the USA.

The early West Coast natives were hunter-gatherers who lived on seafood, game, mushrooms and berries. Spanish missionaries first planted olive trees and vines, orchards and kitchen gardens. Now, ingenious irrigation and intensive cultivation have turned California into an all-year producer and major exporter of an enormous variety of fruits and vegetables, such as peaches, plums, figs, tomatoes, avocados, artichokes and asparagus.

Fishing is a major industry of the Northwest. As well as salmon, the cold waters of the Pacific yield halibut, flounders, herring, rockfish and Pacific cod, prawns, crabs, clams and other shellfish; the crystal-clear rivers and lakes are full of trout, pike and perch. Large areas of Washington and Oregon are forested, making the US a leading timber producer, but fruit—especially apples, pears and berries—as well as wheat are profusely grown.

Such bounty from land and ocean ensures that West Coast cooking is founded on freshness and variety. California is noted for its light, subtle and creative cuisine. Because of its multi-ethnic population, classic American dishes often have, for example, an added French or Oriental nuance and, further south, Mexican influences become stronger. Fish and seafood dishes such as *cioppino* are always favourites, especially around San Francisco.

The West Coast is also a major wine-

growing region. California produces the best known and most exported US wines, especially from the Sonoma and Napa Valleys. Reds include Cabernet Sauvignon, Pinot Noir, Merlot and the native Zinfandel; whites include Chardonnay, Sauvignon Blanc and Gewürztraminer. Visitors are welcome at many of the vineyards.

San Francisco, on the tip of a hilly peninsula between the ocean and San Francisco Bay, is one of the USA's most beautiful and fascinating cities. Brightly coloured houses line the steep hills and cable-cars crisscross the streets. There are many ethnic neighbourhoods and, since the 1970s, an acknowledged gay community.

The largest Chinese population in the Western world lives here, many of them descended from workers brought to build the transcontinental railway. A stroll through Chinatown is a feast for the senses, with displays of exotic foods and the sounds and delicious smells of cooking pervading the air.

The coast road from San Francisco north to Oregon and Washington looks down steep cliffs to little fishing ports, white, sandy beaches and plump sea lions sunning themselves on the rocks.

South of San Francisco, the coast is breathtakingly beautiful, with hidden coves and sheer cliffs pounded by the Pacific surf. Below Santa Cruz is Monterey, where one can watch sea lions and sea otters and visit the Monterey Bay Aquarium or Cannery Row, made famous by John Steinbeck. Further south is modern, multi-ethnic Los Angeles, with its freeways, tall office buildings, Hollywood, Beverley Hills and Sunset Boulevard.

Inland, Yosemite National Park offers spectacular scenery and the highest waterfall in North America. Giant redwoods thrive in the humid, foggy climate of the Coast Ranges and on Sierra Nevada's western slopes. The biggest are in Sequoia National Park.

Victorian villas with brightly painted façades climb a steep street along Alamo Square. They survived San Francisco's devastating 1906 earthquake, after which much of the city was rebuilt.

Alaska and Hawaii

Alaska

Great stretches of uninhabited arctic tundra and coniferous forests, high mountains, glaciers, rugged coasts and a feeling of immense solitude—this is Alaska, the USA's largest but least populated state. Bought from Russia in 1867, the new acquisition was at first ridiculed as "Seward's Polar Bear Garden", after Secretary of State William Henry Seward, who was largely responsible for its purchase. It soon became clear, however, that this was not just a land of polar bears when minerals were discovered.

The Gold Rush, immortalized in Charlie Chaplin's film, opened the territory to new settlers, and soon there was a thriving fishing industry. Alaskan waters are among America's richest fishing grounds, and freshly caught salmon, cod, rockfish, tuna and shellfish are on offer everywhere. Game and wildfowl also appear on the menu. Despite the long, cold winter, many fruits and vegetables thrive, and with almost continuous daylight during the summer, they grow fast and strong.

Alaskan cookery is rustic: hearty, warming stews and roasts in winter; grilled fish, lots of vegetables and berry fruits in summer; and sourdough bread or waffles. Recipes introduced by Russian settlers include *pirozhki*—crisp, filled pastry cases—especially delicious with salmon or crab fillings.

The best times to visit Alaska are early summer or early autumn. The interior can be very hot in mid-summer and there are plagues of mosquitoes. Winters are severe and daylight hours short—although Alaskans enjoy skiing and getting around by snowmobiles or dog sleighs. There are few major roads, but most places can be reached by air. Many tourists arrive by boat via the southern fjords.

There are countless national parks and wilderness areas. North of Alaska's largest city, Anchorage, is Denali National Park, encompassing Mt. McKinley, the nation's highest mountain, where one can see bears, wolves, moose and caribou. In the southeast, there are seals as well as 16 glaciers in Glacier Bay Park, and from the Kenai Peninsula south of Anchorage boats can take one for a close-up view of whales and porpoises.

Hawaii

There could not be a greater contrast to the cool, lonely wilderness of Alaska than sunny, lively Hawaii. These two states have little in common other than that they are both part of the USA and lie outside its mainland borders.

Hawaii, some 3,800 kilometres from San Francisco, is made up of a series of volcanic islands that rose from the ocean floor some five million years ago.

Mt. McKinley towers over the Alaskan interior north of Anchorage. At 6,193 metres, it is the United States' highest mountain.

The warm climate, wonderful beaches, tropical forests, many waterfalls and active volcanoes, as well as the chance to sample the widely ranging cuisine, makes Hawaii irresistible to tourists.

The earliest settlers came from the southern Polynesian islands in about the eighth century. They lived on fish and coconuts, and brought not only taros (potato-like tubers), yams, sweet potatoes and bananas, but also pigs and chickens. The archipelago was discovered by Captain Cook in 1778 (he called it the Sandwich Islands, after the Earl of Sandwich). Christian missionaries followed soon after.

Of the eight main islands, Hawaii, which gives its name to the state, is by far the largest—its other name is "Big Island". Its five volcanoes include Kilauea, one of the world's most active volcanoes. On Oahu island is the busy cosmopolitan state capital, Honolulu, and the internationally famous Waikiki beach resort. Maui has many resorts, wonderful beaches and restaurants,

and a lively nightlife. The pace is slower on Molokai, with its sugar and macadamia nut plantations, and Lanai, once known as pineapple island under its former owners, the Dole Company.

As well as the major pineapple and sugar cane industries, crops grown on the islands' fertile volcanic soil include taros, yams, rice, coffee, bananas and exotic fruits. Fish of all shapes and sizes, and also shellfish, are plentiful.

In the mid-19th century, many Chinese worked on the big American sugar plantations and more recently Japanese, Portuguese, Puerto Ricans, Filipinos and Koreans have settled on the islands, creating a lively ethnic mix and colourful cuisine. The Chinese influence remains strong with stir-fries, sweet-and-sour and noodle dishes. Typical Hawaiian dishes include *poi* (puréed taro), usually served at a *luau*, or festive meal, the focal point of which is a pig filled with hot stones, wrapped in leaves and grilled over hot stones in an *imu*, an oven dug out of the ground.

Waikiki Beach on Oahu, Hawaii's capital island, is a popular destination for American holidaymakers.

For festive occasions, Hawaiian women like to don extravagant headdresses.

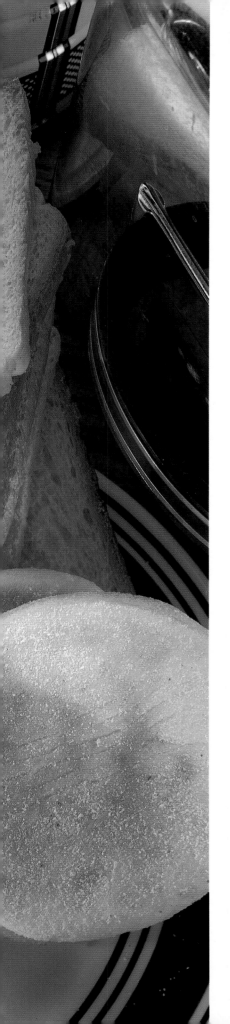

BREAKFASTS AND BRUNCHES

If you have ever been to America and had breakfast in one of the many diners or coffee shops, you will have been astounded at the enormous appetites of those around you. Plates are piled high and the huge portions could make lunch superfluous. Coffee is usually included and the waiter or waitress will refill your cup as often as you wish, free of charge.

Eggs, fried "sunny side up" or "over easy" (*see page 34*) are an essential part of American breakfasts. With the eggs come crisply fried rashers of bacon, boiled ham or sausages. Hash browns (potatoes fried with onion) make a tasty accompaniment. In the South, people eat a porridge-like cereal called hominy grits (made from coarsely ground, treated maize kernels cooked with water or milk), that are sometimes also served with eggs.

Breakfast may also include cereals such as cornflakes, toast with butter and jam and, for the truly ravenous, there are pancakes or waffles with lashings of butter and maple syrup. Or you might prefer bagels, filled perhaps with smoked salmon and cream cheese.

Like so many delightful customs, brunch was an American invention. This combination of late breakfast and early lunch is best enjoyed at the weekend, when anything from blueberry muffins and doughnuts to creamy soup, prawn cocktail, smoked salmon or baked pasta may be added to, or take the place of, the breakfast dishes.

Pancakes with maple syrup

Simple • All regions **Thick, maple-flavoured pancakes** *Serves 4*

125 g plain flour
1 tsp baking powder
1 tsp maple syrup
1 large egg
15 cl milk
salt
butter for frying
maple syrup for serving

**Preparation time: 20 minutes
(plus 30 minutes' standing time)**

890 kJ/210 calories per portion

1 Sift the flour into a bowl. Add the baking powder, maple syrup, egg, milk and a little salt, and stir to a smooth batter with a hand whisk. Cover the bowl and leave the batter to stand at room temperature for 30 minutes.

2 Melt a little butter or margarine in a non-stick frying pan.

3 Using a ladle, pour the batter into the pan, a little at a time, to make about 12 small, thick pancakes. Cook over medium heat until golden-brown on both sides. Serve the hot pancakes lavishly sprinkled with maple syrup.

Variation: French toast

Whisk 2 eggs vigorously with 10 cl milk, 2 tbsp sugar and ½ tsp vanilla essence. Cut 4 slices from a tin loaf, remove the crusts, then cut each slice diagonally in half. In a heavy frying pan, fry 8 rashers of bacon until crisp, then remove and keep warm. Heat 30 g butter in the pan until it froths. Dip the bread triangles briefly in the egg mixture, then fry over medium heat until golden-brown. Lay the bacon on top of the bread, sprinkle with maple syrup and serve immediately.

Note: Hot pancakes are often topped with pats of butter which melt with the heat. Fried bacon rashers are another favourite accompaniment. You can also mix blueberries, diced apple or nuts straight into the batter.

Maple syrup

This golden, delicately-flavoured syrup is a favourite with North Americans who pour it lavishly on waffles and pancakes, and use it to flavour ice cream, desserts and cakes. It is made from the sap of the sugar maple (*Acer saccharum*) and, to a lesser extent, the black maple (*Acer nigrum*) which flourish in northeastern USA and in Canada.

The best time to tap maples is in the thaw following a freeze, when the sap runs most freely. To obtain the flavour and thick consistency of syrup, it needs to be drastically reduced by boiling. An average yield of 40 litres of sap from one tree will produce only about 1 litre of syrup.

The American Indians taught the

first settlers how to bore holes in the tree trunks and collect the sap over several weeks. To boil the sap, the Indians put it in wooden vessels and added hot stones.

The best syrup is obtained from the season's first, carefully processed, tappings. The paler the syrup, the more

delicate and aromatic the flavour will be. Later tappings often need more intense heat treatment to thicken the sap. Though cheaper, these syrups tend to be dark brown, with a strong caramel taste that can almost completely mask the maple syrup flavour.

Blueberry muffins

Not difficult • New England **American muffins made with blueberries** *Makes 12 muffins*

100 g butter, softened, plus a little
extra for greasing the tins
175 g sugar
2 eggs
few drops of vanilla essence
salt
250 g plain flour
2 tsp baking powder
150 g buttermilk
225 g blueberries

*Preparation time: 20 minutes
(plus 35 minutes' baking time)*

1,000 kJ/240 calories per muffin

1 Preheat the oven to 180°C (350°F or Mark 4). Grease several muffin tins.

2 Place the butter or margarine in a bowl, add the sugar and beat until pale and creamy. Stir in the eggs, vanilla essence and salt.

3 Sift the flour and baking powder into a bowl. Add some of the buttermilk, then a little of the egg mixture, beating well between each addition. Continue adding them alternately until used up.

4 Wash and dry the blueberries, and fold them carefully into the dough.

5 Pour the dough into the greased muffin tins. Bake in the centre of the oven for about 35 minutes.

Variation: The muffins are delicious if you stir 200 to 225 g strawberries (wild ones, if you can get them) into the dough instead of blueberries. Mix the dough with ordinary milk in place of buttermilk, if preferred.

Note: If you do not have a muffin tin, simply bake the muffin mixture in paper cake cases.

Doughnuts

Fairly easy • All regions **Ring-shaped doughnuts** *Makes 18 doughnuts*

50 g butter, softened
3 eggs
150 g sugar
20 cl milk
few drops of vanilla essence
salt
freshly grated nutmeg
625 to 650 g plain flour
20 g baking powder
vegetable oil for deep frying
caster sugar for coating

Preparation time: 1 hour

1,100 kJ/260 calories per doughnut

1 Beat the butter, eggs and sugar together in a bowl until creamy, then stir in the milk, vanilla essence and a little salt and nutmeg.

2 Sift the flour and baking powder together into a bowl. Gradually stir the flour into the egg mixture, using the pastry hook attachment of a hand mixer, then knead the dough.

3 On a floured surface, roll out the dough to a thickness of about 1 cm. Using a doughnut cutter, cut the pastry into rings. If you do not have one of these cutters, use a pastry cutter or a glass, about 7 cm in diameter, to cut out circles. Use a pastry cutter or glass about 3 cm in diameter to cut out the middle of the pastry circles, to make ring-shaped doughnuts.

4 Heat the oil in a deep, heavy-based saucepan until bubbles rise from a wooden chopstick dipped in the oil. If using an electric deep-fryer, heat to 180°C (350°F).

5 Fry the doughnuts in batches until golden-brown all over. If necessary, hollow out the holes in the centre with the handle of a wooden spoon.

6 Remove the doughnuts from the fat with a slotted spoon and drain them thoroughly on paper towels. Roll them in the caster sugar and serve at once.

Note: It is worth looking out for the special cutters for making doughnuts with a hole in the middle in specialist cookware shops, as they make cutting the dough much easier.

Bagels

Ring-shaped yeast rolls

¼ *litre milk*
50 *g butter*
1 *tsp salt*
1 *tbsp sugar*
20 *g fresh yeast*
1 *egg white*
about 400 g plain flour
1 *egg yolk*
200 *g smoked salmon or lox*
200 *g full fat cream cheese*
capers (optional)
chopped onions (optional)

*Preparation time: 1½ hours
(plus 20 minutes' cooling time
and 1¼ hours' rising time)*

420 kJ/100 calories per bagel

1 Pour the milk into a saucepan and add the butter, salt and sugar. Bring to the boil, stirring constantly, until the butter has melted. Pour the mixture into a bowl and leave it to cool for about 20 minutes, until lukewarm.

2 Crumble the yeast into the mixture, and stir until dissolved. Cover the mixture and leave to stand for about 10 minutes, until it starts to bubble. Lightly whisk the egg white in a cup or bowl, then beat it into the mixture.

3 Work the plain flour into the yeast mixture a little at a time, and knead to a very soft, smooth dough. Continue to knead the dough for about 10 minutes, until it is no longer sticky, then cover and leave to rise in a warm place for about 1 hour.

4 Shape the dough into 20 balls about the size of a chicken's egg (about 40 g in weight). Push your index finger right through the middle of each ball of dough to make a ring shape (*above*).

5 On a lightly floured work surface, turn each ring with your index finger inside the hole, until the hole measures about 3 cm in diameter (*above*).

6 Leave the shaped bagels to prove on the work surface, covered with a cloth, for another 10 minutes. Meanwhile, preheat the oven to 200°C (400°F or Mark 6).

7 Bring plenty of water to the boil in a large saucepan. Add the bagels to the boiling water, three or four at a time, and parboil them for no more than 1 minute. Remove them from the water with a slotted spoon, drain thoroughly, then arrange on two baking sheets lined with greaseproof paper.

8 Whisk the egg yolk with 2 tbsp cold water, and use it to brush the bagels. Bake each batch of bagels in the centre of the oven for 15 minutes. Serve the bagels with the smoked salmon and cream cheese. If wished, garnish each bagel with 1 tsp each of capers and chopped onion.

Note: In America, bagels are just as popular for lunch as for breakfast. They can be sprinkled with poppy or sesame seeds, or with a little coarse salt, before baking, if wished.

Eggs with hash browns

Simple • All regions   **Fried eggs with potatoes and onions**   *Serves 4*

700 g cold, boiled potatoes
1 large onion
125 g thin rashers smoked streaky
bacon
40 to 60 g butter
salt
freshly ground black pepper
4 to 8 eggs

Preparation time: 30 minutes

2,800 kJ/670 calories per portion

1 Peel the potatoes, if necessary, and cut them into 2 to 3 cm dice. Peel and finely chop the onion. Cut the bacon into thin strips.

2 Put 30 g of the butter in a large non-stick frying pan, add the bacon strips and fry over medium heat until they are lightly browned.

3 Add the diced potatoes and chopped onion, season with salt and pepper, and fry until the potato dice are crisp and brown on all sides.

4 While the potatoes are cooking, fry the eggs in the remaining butter in one or two other large frying pans.

5 Serve the hash browns with the eggs on top, accompanied by crisp rashers of bacon and hot toast, if wished.

Note: In America, eggs fried in the usual way are called "sunny side up". If the eggs are flipped over and fried on both sides, Americans call them "over easy". Sausages, rashers of bacon or ham are often served with eggs and hash browns.

Leftover boiled potatoes are ideal for this dish. Alternatively, boil the required quantity for 20 to 30 minutes in salted water and leave them to cool thoroughly before making hash browns.

Red flannel hash

Simple • New England

Fried chopped beetroot, potatoes and carrots

Serves 4 to 6

3 cooked beetroot
4 small cooked potatoes
2 small cooked carrots
1 medium-sized onion
½ small sweet pepper
300 g corned beef
100 g smoked streaky bacon
30 g butter
salt
freshly ground black pepper
15 g parsley

Preparation time: 20 minutes

1,000 kJ/240 calories per portion
(if serving 6)

1 Chop the cooked vegetables into small pieces. Peel the onion, wash the pepper and remove the ribs and seeds. Chop the onion, pepper and the corned beef into small pieces. Dice the bacon.

2 Heat the butter in a large frying pan and fry the bacon over medium heat until it is crisp and the fat runs. Stir in the rest of the prepared ingredients.

3 Fry the hash over low heat for about 5 to 10 minutes, until heated through.

4 Season the ingredients in the pan with salt and pepper. Wash the parsley and shake it dry. Chop finely and then sprinkle it over the cooked hash and serve, accompanied by toast.

Note: Served with fried or poached eggs, this is a popular breakfast or brunch dish throughout America. In New England, it traditionally appears on the breakfast table when there are leftovers from the previous day's New England boiled dinner (*see page 114*). Nowadays, it is made with canned corned beef instead of home-made.

If you do not have any leftover vegetables, boil the beetroot for about 40 minutes in salted water, the potatoes for 20 to 30 minutes and the carrots for about 10 minutes. Leave the vegetables until they are completely cold before mixing them with the other ingredients or they will quickly fall apart and look unappetizing.

Sourdough waffles

Waffles made with a traditional sourdough

Takes time • Alaska

Makes 8 waffles

For the sourdough starter:
150 g plain flour
3.5 g dried yeast

For the sourdough:
200 g plain flour

For the waffles on baking day:
1 egg
7 tbsp vegetable oil, plus extra for greasing
4 tbsp milk or double cream
2 tbsp sugar
1 tsp baking powder
½ tsp salt

**Preparation time: 1 hour
(plus 2 days' proving time)**

1,100 kJ/260 calories per waffle

1 For the starter, place the 150 g flour in a bowl. Make a well in the middle of the flour and sprinkle the dried yeast into the well. Pour in ¼ litre warm water, at about 43°C (110°F), and stir to a smooth dough.

2 Completely cover the bowl with a cloth and leave the dough to stand for 24 hours at room temperature, away from draughts (in an unlit oven, for example). If, at the end of this time, the dough has not produced plenty of bubbles, you will have to start again.

3 The next day, gradually stir ¼ litre hand-hot water and the 200 g flour into the sourdough starter. Cover and leave to rise at room temperature for a further 12 hours (*above*). The dough must also produce lots of bubbles at this stage, otherwise it is unusable.

4 Divide the sourdough in half. Place one half of the dough in a freezer container and store in the refrigerator to use another time.

5 Add the egg, the 7 tbsp oil, the milk or cream, sugar, baking powder and salt to the other half of the sourdough, and stir to make a smooth batter.

6 Heat a lidded waffle iron to medium setting, following the manufacturer's instructions. If necessary, brush both surfaces thinly with oil. (Non-stick appliances usually only need to be greased the first time they are used.)

7 For each waffle, spread 2 to 3 tbsp of batter over the bottom half of the iron. Close the lid and bake until golden-brown. Cook the waffles one at a time until all the batter is used up.

8 Serve the waffles freshly cooked, spread with butter, marmalade or jam, whichever you prefer.

Variation: For a quicker version, you can make waffles with baking powder. Mix about 300 g flour, 1 tsp baking powder, a little salt and sugar, ½ litre buttermilk and 3 egg yolks. Fold in the stiffly beaten whites of 3 eggs and then prepare the waffles as in the recipe.

Note: In Alaska and along America's West Coast, sourdough is used for making waffles, pancakes and speciality breads. In the old days, the sourdough starter used to be made with potato water, but now the usual way is with dried yeast.

It takes time to make sourdough, but once the starter is ready, it will keep almost indefinitely. Part of the dough is put into a freezer container, firmly sealed and placed in the refrigerator. If it is topped up weekly with the flour and water mixture (as described in Step 3, above), it will keep for years. Connoisseurs claim that a sourdough improves with age.

SALADS AND STARTERS

Americans love salads. All over
the United States salads are
served as starters, side dishes
accompanying meat or fish, or on their
own as a lunchtime main course.

One story has it that Columbus, on
his second voyage, took lettuce seeds
to the New World. Green salad,
however, has never been very popular
with Americans. When they talk about
salad, they are more likely to mean
coleslaw—the Dutch settlers' *koolsla*—
or a colourful blend of different kinds
of ingredients, of which lettuce is just
one. Some American salads, such as
Caesar salad, Waldorf salad and
three-bean salad (cooked dried beans
of differing type and colour in a
vinaigrette dressing), have rightly
become internationally famous.

Many restaurants offer large salad
buffets, where customers choose their
own selection of salads and dressings.
A salad buffet is also easy to prepare
at home: a crisp iceberg lettuce, a few
juicy tomatoes, cucumber, spring
onions, young carrots, sweet peppers,
sweetcorn, celery—the more colourful
and varied the choice, the better.

Apart from salads, some of the most
delicious starters, also popular as
snacks, are made with seafood. They
include steamed mussels and clams,
oysters served raw or baked *au gratin*,
and grilled prawns (in America called
shrimp, whatever their size) or spicy
seafood cocktails. There are as many
imaginative ways of preparing seafood
as there are delicious foods in the sea.

Waldorf salad

Celery, walnut and apple salad

Serves 4

1 very fresh egg yolk
3 tbsp lemon juice
12.5 cl vegetable oil
3 to 4 tbsp milk or cream
salt
freshly ground white pepper
3 sticks celery
50 g shelled walnuts
3 firm, tart apples
4 to 8 lettuce leaves (optional)

Preparation time: 30 minutes

1,900 kJ/450 calories per portion

1 Mix the egg yolk and 1 tbsp of the lemon juice in a deep bowl. Add the vegetable oil, drop by drop at first, then pouring it into the emulsion in a thin stream, stirring vigorously to make a creamy mayonnaise. Stir the milk or cream into the mayonnaise, and season to taste with a little salt and white pepper.

2 Wash and thinly slice the celery, removing any stringy bits. Chop the shelled walnuts.

3 Wash and polish the apples, or peel them, if preferred. Cut into quarters, remove the core, then chop them into dice, about 3 cm. Sprinkle immediately with the rest of the lemon juice.

4 Mix all the ingredients together and adjust the seasoning, if necessary. Serve immediately, either in a bowl, or on a bed of lettuce.

Variation: Raisins, grapes or finely chopped pineapple can be added to the salad.

Note: Waldorf salad was created at the end of the 19th century at New York's luxury Waldorf-Astoria hotel.
   Make sure you use only a very fresh egg from a reliable source for this recipe—uncooked eggs can carry the salmonella bacteria that causes food poisoning.

Coleslaw

Cabbage and carrot salad

Serves 4

4 tbsp white wine vinegar
1 tbsp sugar
1 tbsp flour
1 tsp dry mustard
1 tsp salt
4 tbsp double cream
15 g butter
2 eggs
400 g white cabbage
1 medium-sized carrot

**Preparation time: 30 minutes
(plus 3 hours' standing time)**

860 kJ/200 calories per portion

1 Pour 5 cl water into a saucepan, add the vinegar, sugar, flour, mustard and salt, and mix thoroughly.

2 Bring the mixture to the boil over low heat, stirring constantly. Add the cream and butter, and continue to stir until the butter has melted.

3 Whisk the eggs in a cup or bowl. Stir 2 to 3 tbsp of the hot liquid into the whisked eggs, then pour the mixture back into the pan and stir thoroughly. Continue to stir until the mixture thickens, then pour it into a bowl.

4 Trim, wash and grate or shred the white cabbage. Peel and coarsely grate the carrot. Add the vegetables to the dressing and season to taste. Leave to stand for 2 to 3 hours before serving.

Note: All over the United States, coleslaw is served with steak and baked or fried fish. Sometimes leek rings are added. Coleslaw can also be made with ready-made mayonnaise, or a mixture of mayonnaise and soured cream or yoghurt.

Caesar salad

Not difficult • California

Green salad with bacon, Parmesan and croûtons

Serves 4

75 g rindless, smoked streaky bacon
2 slices from a white tin loaf
2 to 3 garlic cloves
6 tbsp vegetable oil
1 large cos lettuce
2 very fresh eggs (see Note,
page 40)
10 cl virgin olive oil
3 to 4 tbsp lemon juice
salt
freshly ground black pepper
2 anchovy fillets
30 g Parmesan cheese, in one piece

Preparation time: 30 minutes

2,700 kJ/640 calories per portion

1 Dice the bacon and fry it in a wide frying pan over low heat until crisp. Meanwhile, cut the bread into 1 cm cubes, discarding the crusts if wished. Peel and chop the garlic.

2 Remove the bacon from the pan, and set aside. Heat the oil in the pan, add the bread and fry over medium heat until golden-brown on all sides. Just before they are done, add the garlic. Drain the croûtons on paper towels.

3 Trim and wash the cos lettuce, then drain thoroughly or spin dry in a salad spinner. Cut the leaves crosswise into strips about 2 cm wide.

4 Bring some water to the boil in a small saucepan. Prick the eggshells and place the eggs in the boiling water for about 1 minute. Remove them from the pan and rinse in cold water. Break open the shells, then use a teaspoon to scoop the eggs straight from the shells into a bowl.

5 Add the olive oil and lemon juice a little at a time, then whisk vigorously with a hand whisk to make a dressing. Season with salt and pepper, then toss the salad in the dressing.

6 Rinse the anchovy fillets under cold running water, then dry and chop into small pieces. Thinly slice or coarsely grate the Parmesan cheese.

7 Stir the anchovies and bacon into the salad, sprinkle the croûtons and Parmesan cheese on top, and serve the salad immediately.

Chicken salad

Not difficult • The South

Cold chicken in a creamy sauce

Serves 4

1 kg oven-ready chicken
1 leek • 1 carrot
50 to 75 g piece of celeriac
15 g fresh parsley
1 tbsp black peppercorns
5 tbsp double cream
10 cl cider vinegar
2 egg yolks
1 tbsp flour
1 to 2 tbsp sugar
½ tbsp dry mustard • salt
freshly ground white pepper
2 sticks celery
2 spring onions
2 tbsp lemon juice
lettuce or celery leaves (optional)

Preparation time: 1½ hours
(plus 1 to 2 hours' cooling time)

1,600 kJ/380 calories per portion

1 Wash the chicken and place it in a large saucepan or stockpot with just enough hot water to cover. Wash and coarsely chop the leek. Wash, peel and chop the carrot and celeriac, then add the vegetables to the pan. Wash the parsley, shake dry and add to the pan with the peppercorns.

2 Bring the water to the boil, then simmer the chicken over low heat, with the lid half covering the saucepan, for about 45 minutes, until cooked.

3 Remove the chicken from the stock and allow to cool a little. Reserve the stock. Remove the skin and bones and cut the meat into 2 to 3 cm dice. Cover and leave in the refrigerator.

4 In a pan, mix 5 tbsp of the chicken stock with the cream, vinegar, egg yolks, flour, sugar, and mustard, and stir until smooth. Bring to the boil, stirring constantly, and cook until the sauce thickens. Season with salt and pepper, then leave to cool at room temperature for 1 to 2 hours.

5 Meanwhile, wash and trim the celery and spring onions, removing any tough stringy bits from the celery. Thinly slice the celery and spring onions, stir them into the chicken, and sprinkle with lemon juice. Taste the sauce and adjust the seasoning, if necessary, then drizzle it over the chicken. Serve the salad on a bed of lettuce or celery leaves, if wished.

Salad buffet

Salad selection with a choice of dressings

Not difficult · All regions

Serves 8

1 iceberg lettuce
1 small head of celery
250 g tomatoes
1 bunch spring onions
200 g carrots
1 can sweetcorn (285 g drained weight)
100 g bean sprouts
100 g rindless, smoked streaky bacon
3 slices white bread
2 tbsp vegetable oil
3 eggs
30 g fresh chives
3 tbsp sunflower seeds
100 g Cheddar cheese, grated

For the blue cheese dressing:
100 g mild blue cheese
1 garlic clove
100 g crème fraîche
salt
freshly ground white pepper
2 tbsp virgin olive oil

For the French dressing:
4 tbsp wine vinegar
salt
freshly ground black pepper
1 tsp prepared mustard
16 tbsp virgin olive oil

For the thousand island dressing:
75 g mayonnaise
2 tbsp tomato ketchup
1 small egg
1 small sweet red pepper
15 g fresh parsley
a few drops of Tabasco sauce

Preparation time: 1 hour

2,800 kJ/660 calories per portion

1 Trim and wash the iceberg lettuce. Drain thoroughly or spin dry in a salad spinner. Wash the celery, removing any tough stringy bits, and cut it into thin strips. Wash the tomatoes and cut into quarters or eighths.

2 Wash and trim the spring onions, and cut them into thin rings. Peel and coarsely grate the carrots.

3 Drain the sweetcorn. Place the bean sprouts in a colander, rinse under cold running water and drain thoroughly.

4 Cut the bacon into small dice and discard any gristle. Place in a frying pan and fry over medium heat until the fat runs and the bacon is crisp.

5 Cut the bread into small cubes. Remove the bacon from the pan and drain on paper towels. Heat the oil in the pan and fry the bread cubes over medium heat until golden-brown. Drain the croûtons on paper towels.

6 Hard boil the eggs—including the egg for the thousand island dressing. This will take about 10 minutes. Rinse in cold water and remove the shells. Set aside the egg for the thousand island dressing and cut the others into eighths. Wash the chives, pat dry and snip into small pieces.

7 Arrange all the salad ingredients in suitable serving bowls or dishes, with the sunflower seeds and grated cheese in separate small bowls.

8 To make the blue cheese dressing, place the blue cheese in a bowl and mash with a fork. Peel and crush the garlic and mix it into the cheese with the crème fraîche, salt, pepper and olive oil, and stir thoroughly.

9 For the French dressing, whisk the vinegar with salt, pepper and mustard, then stir in the olive oil.

10 To make the thousand island dressing, mix together the mayonnaise and tomato ketchup. Chop the egg. Trim, wash and finely chop the sweet pepper. Wash the parsley, shake it dry and chop finely. Add the chopped ingredients to the mayonnaise mixture and season with the Tabasco sauce.

11 Transfer the dressings to small, individual serving bowls and arrange them beside the salad ingredients. Everyone can make up their own salad with the dressing of their choice.

Variations: Salad buffets are found all over the States. Many fast food chains now have them too. The choice is often enormous. As well as the ingredients suggested here, the buffet might also include beetroot, sprouts of all kinds, beans, broccoli, cauliflower, shredded white cabbage, leeks, cucumber or fruit, pumpkin seeds, sesame seeds, nuts, olives or tuna fish.

Italian dressing is also popular. To make it, stir finely chopped garlic, paprika and chopped fresh herbs into a French dressing. Cream or soured cream and/or tomato ketchup is sometimes added to French dressing.

Lomi lomi

Quick · Hawaii   **Gravlax salad**   *Serves 4*

500 g firm, ripe tomatoes
½ bunch spring onions
125 g gravlax (cured salmon), well chilled

Preparation time: 15 minutes

380 kJ/90 calories per portion

1 Wash the tomatoes and cut them in half, remove the seeds and cut the flesh into small dice.

2 Wash and trim the spring onions and cut into thin rings. Cut the gravlax into fine strips. Mix all the ingredients together and serve immediately.

Variation: This delicate salmon salad is sometimes served with a dressing. Place 1 tsp sugar and 2 to 3 tbsp rice vinegar in a bowl and stir until the sugar has dissolved. Stir 2 tbsp lime or lemon juice and 2 to 3 tbsp sunflower oil into the vinegar. Season with a little dry mustard, salt and pepper, and pour it over the salad. With this variation, it is vital that all the ingredients should be well chilled.

Note: The word *lomi* means something like "massage" in the local Hawaiian dialect. Traditional recipes for this salad use salted salmon, soaked overnight and then "massaged" to make it tender. In Hawaii, *lomi lomi* is one of the dishes served at a *luau*, or traditional celebratory feast.

Shrimp cocktail

Simple · Louisiana   **Prawns in a spicy dressing**   *Serves 4*

3 sprigs fresh parsley
1 stick celery
3 spring onions
1 tbsp coarse-grain, medium-hot mustard
3 tbsp white wine vinegar
10 cl virgin olive oil
salt
freshly ground white pepper
cayenne pepper
400 g cooked, peeled prawns

Preparation time: 20 minutes
(plus 2 hours' marinating time)

1,100 kJ/260 calories per portion

1 Wash the parsley, shake it dry and chop finely. Wash the celery and remove any tough strings. Wash and trim the spring onions. Thinly slice the celery and spring onions.

2 Mix the mustard, vinegar and oil in a bowl. Stir in the chopped parsley and the sliced celery and spring onions. Season generously with salt, white pepper and cayenne pepper to make a piquant dressing.

3 Rinse the prawns under cold running water and pat dry with paper towels. Mix them with the other ingredients, then cover and leave to marinate in the refrigerator for about 2 hours.

Variation: Americans also like to eat prawns (called shrimp in the USA) with a highly seasoned *remoulade* sauce— Creole mustard *(see Note, below)* and paprika whisked into a vinaigrette with the addition of chopped spring onions, celery and parsley.

Note: Mustard is a favourite ingredient in Creole cooking. This usually means a hot, coarse-grain mustard, sold in the United States as "Creole mustard". Any coarse hot or medium-hot mustard can be used instead.

The cuisines of Louisiana and the other Southern states boast a whole range of recipes using prawns. Not for nothing is Biloxi, a little town on the coast of the State of Mississippi, known as the "shrimp capital of the world".

Oysters Rockefeller

Not difficult • Louisiana

Oysters topped with herb and spinach purée

Serves 4

3 spring onions
½ stick celery
15 g fresh parsley
1 small sprig fresh tarragon
200 g leaf spinach
100 g butter
30 g fresh breadcrumbs
a few drops of Tabasco sauce
1 to 2 tbsp anise-flavoured liqueur
(such as anisette)
1 tbsp lemon juice
salt
coarse salt for the baking dish(es)
24 freshly opened oysters

Preparation time: 35 minutes

1,200 kJ/290 calories per portion

1 Wash and trim the spring onions. Wash the celery, pulling off any tough strings. Finely chop the spring onions and celery. Wash the parsley and tarragon, shake dry and chop finely.

2 Trim any withered leaves and tough stalks from the spinach and rinse in two or three changes of cold water. Shake thoroughly dry and chop finely.

3 Preheat the oven to 200°C (400°F or Mark 6). Heat 30 g of the butter in a frying pan and stir-fry the chopped spring onions and celery over low heat for about 3 minutes.

4 Add the chopped herbs and spinach and stir-fry for a further 3 minutes.

5 Purée the fried vegetable mixture in a blender or food processor. Stir the remaining butter and the breadcrumbs into the purée. Add the Tabasco sauce, liqueur and lemon juice, and season to taste with salt.

6 Sprinkle one round ovenproof dish, (or several small ovenproof dishes) with coarse salt. Arrange the opened oysters in their shells in the dish and top each one with a little of the herb and spinach purée. Bake in the centre of the oven for 8 to 10 minutes.

Note: This dish was first served in 1899, at Antoine's Restaurant in New Orleans. Since then, it has become an American household favourite.

Steamed clams

Clams served with their own stock and butter

Serves 4

3 kg live clams or 2 to 3 kg mussels
2 medium-sized onions
15 g fresh parsley
250 g butter
1 garlic clove

Preparation time: 1 hour

2,300 kJ/550 calories per portion

1 Wash and scrub the clams or mussels under cold running water. Tap sharply any shells that are open and discard any that do not close.

2 Peel and finely chop the onions. Wash the parsley, shake it dry and chop finely.

3 Melt 60 g butter in a wide pan over medium heat and fry the onions for about 5 minutes, until transparent, then stir in the chopped parsley. Peel and crush the garlic and add it to the pan. Pour in ¾ litre water and bring to the boil.

4 Add the clams, cover with a lid and steam them over high heat for about 5 to 8 minutes, shaking the pan occasionally, until they open. Discard any that remain closed.

5 Melt the rest of the butter in a small saucepan over low heat. Meanwhile, using a slotted spoon, transfer the cooked clams from the pan to a warm deep serving bowl.

6 Strain the clam stock through a fine sieve and divide it between four small bowls. Pour the melted butter into a further four small bowls.

7 Place the clams on the table and give each guest a soup plate, one bowl of melted butter and another of clam stock. To eat the steamed clams, detach each clam from the shell with a fork, dip it first in the stock, then in the butter. Serve the clams with fresh green salad and crusty white bread.

SOUPS AND STEWS

T here is scarcely any food that American cooks do not turn into a light broth, thick cream soup or chunky stew. Among the most common ingredients for both soups and stews are sweetcorn, pumpkin and seafood, simply because these have always been the most widely available.

Each region has developed its own soup specialities—peanut soup and black bean soup in the south, creamy clam chowder in the east, bisques and sumptuous gumbos in Louisiana.

The first instant soups were invented at the end of the 19th century. To sustain them on their long journey, travelling westwards on horseback or by wagon, the pioneers developed a kind of bouillon cube which they could simply mix with hot water to make a warm, satisfying meal in minutes. Hardworking pioneer homesteaders often used to eat soup for breakfast.

The American Indians cooked their food all in one pot—in their case a hollowed-out pumpkin shell—a method they passed on to the early settlers. In those days, each family owned only a single cooking pot, so one-pot stews were the ideal solution. Everything edible ended up in the huge iron pot suspended over the fire which was left to cook for hours on end, until even the toughest pieces of meat were tender.

Some of the earliest traditional stews, such as Boston baked beans or the chicken and vegetable Brunswick stew, are still popular today.

Chilled avocado soup

Simple • Florida

Spicy avocado and coriander soup

Serves 4

1 small carrot
1 medium-sized onion
1 small tomato
1 sprig parsley
1 small garlic clove
1 bay leaf
1 tsp black peppercorns
2 ripe avocados
2 to 4 tbsp white wine vinegar
a few drops of Tabasco sauce
salt
freshly ground white pepper
4 to 5 sprigs coriander

Preparation time: 45 minutes
(plus 4 hours' chilling time)

1,100 kJ/260 calories per portion

1 Peel the carrot and onion. Halve the tomato and remove the seeds. Finely chop all the vegetables.

2 Wash the parsley, shake it dry and chop finely. Peel the garlic clove and cut it into four pieces.

3 Place the chopped vegetables in a saucepan with the parsley, garlic, bay leaf and peppercorns, and add ¾ litre water. Bring to the boil, then reduce the heat and simmer over low heat, with the lid half covering the saucepan, for about 30 minutes. Strain the stock through a fine sieve into a large bowl and leave it to get cold.

4 Halve the avocados lengthwise and remove the stones. Scoop the flesh out of the shells with a spoon and put it in a blender or food processor. Purée the avocado flesh immediately, adding some of the chilled vegetable stock.

5 Stir the avocado purée into the rest of the stock. Season with vinegar, Tabasco sauce, salt and pepper. Wash the coriander, shake dry, then chop it and stir into the soup.

6 Leave the soup in the refrigerator for about 3 to 4 hours to chill, then serve it well chilled.

Variation: Substitute flat-leaf parsley for the coriander. Although the two herbs look very similar, the flavour of the soup will be quite different.

Clam chowder

Creamy clam and potato soup

Fairly easy • New England

Serves 4

1.4 kg live clams (about 7.5 cm in diameter) or Venus mussels
600 g floury potatoes
salt
50 g rindless, smoked streaky bacon
1 medium-sized onion
¼ litre milk
15 g butter, straight from the refrigerator
1 tbsp flour
200 g double cream
15 g parsley
2 sprigs thyme
freshly ground white pepper

Preparation time: 1 hour

1,900 kJ/450 calories per portion

1 Wash and scrub the clams or mussels under cold running water. Tap sharply any shells that are open, then discard those that do not close.

2 Bring ¼ litre water to the boil in a large saucepan. Add the clams and cook over high heat for 4 to 5 minutes, until the shells open. Discard any that remain closed. Drain through a sieve and reserve the cooking stock. Remove the clams from their shells and chop them coarsely.

3 Peel the potatoes and cut them into small cubes. Bring about 2 litres lightly salted water to the boil and parboil the potatoes for about 3 minutes, then drain off the water.

4 Finely dice the bacon, removing any gristle. Peel and finely chop the onion.

Fry the bacon and onion in a wide pan over low heat until the bacon fat runs and the onion is transparent.

5 Stir in the milk and potatoes. Bring to the boil, then cover and simmer for about 5 minutes.

6 Blend the butter and flour together with a fork, then stir the mixture into the hot soup, a small piece at a time. Add the cream and continue to simmer, covered, over low heat for about 10 minutes.

7 Wash the parsley and thyme, shake dry, chop and stir into the soup. Add the clams and cooking stock, season with salt and pepper, and return briefly to the boil before serving.

Peanut soup

Simple • Virginia

Creamy, Southern-style peanut soup

Serves 4

1 stick celery
1 medium-sized onion
60 g butter
1 ½ tbsp flour
¾ litre chicken stock
125 g peanut butter
salt
freshly ground black pepper
1 to 2 tbsp lemon juice
2 tbsp unsalted, roasted peanuts

Preparation time: 30 minutes

1,600 kJ/380 calories per portion

1 Wash the celery, removing any tough strings. Peel the onion. Finely chop the celery and onion.

2 Melt the butter in a wide pan and stir-fry the chopped celery and onion over medium heat for about 3 minutes, until the onion has softened.

3 Sprinkle the flour over the celery and onion, and fry briefly to cook the flour, then stir in the chicken stock a little at a time.

4 Add the peanut butter and simmer over low heat for about 10 minutes, stirring the mixture constantly.

5 Season the soup with salt, pepper and lemon juice. Coarsely chop the peanuts and sprinkle them over the soup just before serving.

Note: Peanut butter is made from roasted, ground peanuts which are mixed with salt and vegetable oil. In many cases, sugar is also added. Americans use it both as a spread and as a culinary ingredient. In the deep South, peanut soup is often spiced up with cayenne pepper or crushed red pepper flakes.

Peanuts

Native to tropical South America, peanuts were introduced to North America by the Spaniards early in the 17th century and a hundred years later were being cultivated commercially in Georgia. Now peanuts are a major American crop.

The peanut is not really a nut but a pulse, like peas, beans and lentils. Unlike other members of the leguminous family, however, the fruit grows underground—hence its alternative name, groundnut.

The plant grows to a height of 30 to 60 cm. After flowering, tendrils called "pegs" develop from the withered flower heads and push themselves several centimetres into the ground, and it is here that the peanuts develop.

Five months of warm weather are needed to grow peanuts successfully. When the peanuts are ripe, the whole plants are removed from the soil and left to dry in the sun for several days before processing. About half of the USA's crops go into the making of peanut butter—that great American sandwich staple—the rest are roasted and salted as a snack food, processed into oil or used to feed livestock such as pigs.

Black bean soup

Spicy bean and vegetable soup

Takes time • The South

Serves 4

200 g dried black beans
1 medium-sized onion
1 carrot • 1 stick celery
15 g butter • 1 garlic clove
¾ litre chicken stock
100 g rindless, smoked streaky
bacon • 1 bay leaf
ground cloves • ground mace
cayenne pepper
1 tbsp white wine vinegar
1 tbsp dry sherry • salt
1 unwaxed lemon
cress for garnish

Preparation time: 30 minutes
(plus 2 hours' cooking time and
12 hours' soaking time)

1,600 kJ/380 calories per portion

1 Place the beans in a bowl and cover with water. Leave to soak overnight.

2 Peel the onion and carrot. Wash the celery, pulling off any tough strings. Finely chop all the vegetables.

3 Heat the butter in a wide pan and stir-fry the chopped vegetables over medium heat for about 5 minutes.

4 Peel and crush the garlic. Stir it into the vegetables, then add the stock.

5 Drain the beans, then put them in a saucepan with enough cold water to cover. Bring to the boil and boil rapidly for 10 minutes, then drain and add to the vegetables with the bacon. Season

with the bay leaf, ground cloves and mace, and the cayenne pepper. Bring to the boil, then cover and simmer over low heat for about 2 hours, until the beans are completely tender.

6 Remove the bacon and the bay leaf. Purée the soup in a food processor or blender and return it to the saucepan.

7 Bring the mixture back to the boil. Add the vinegar, sherry and salt. Taste and add a little more of the spices, if necessary. If the soup is too thick, add a little water to dilute it.

8 Peel and thinly slice the lemon. Arrange the slices on top of the soup with the cress. Serve hot.

Corn chowder

Thick sweetcorn and chicken soup

Not difficult • New England

Serves 4

50 g smoked streaky bacon
1 tbsp vegetable oil
1 baby leek
1 stick celery
½ litre chicken stock
2 small waxy potatoes
1 can sweetcorn (185 g drained
weight)
200 g chicken breast fillet
10 cl double cream
salt
freshly ground white pepper
15 g chives

Preparation time: 45 minutes

1,400 kJ/330 calories per portion

1 Remove the bacon rind and finely chop the bacon. Heat the oil in a large saucepan and fry the bacon over low heat until the fat runs.

2 Wash and trim the leek and celery. Remove any tough strings from the celery. Thinly slice both vegetables.

3 Add them to the pan and stir-fry for about 2 minutes over low heat, then add the chicken stock.

4 Peel, wash and dice the potatoes. Add to the soup and simmer, covered, over low heat for about 15 minutes.

5 Drain the sweetcorn. Reserve half of it and purée the remainder. Cut the chicken breast into thin strips.

6 Add the reserved whole sweetcorn and the sweetcorn purée, the chicken strips and the cream to the soup. Season with salt and pepper and cook for a further 5 minutes.

7 Wash the chives, shake them dry, cut into small pieces and sprinkle over the soup just before serving.

Pumpkin soup

Spicy pumpkin soup

Serves 4

1 pumpkin, weighing about 900 g
(or 600 g trimmed pumpkin flesh)
50 g butter
1 tbsp brown sugar
¾ litre milk
½ tsp ground mace
freshly grated nutmeg
ground cloves
salt
freshly ground white pepper

Preparation time: 45 minutes

1,100 kJ/260 calories per portion

1 Peel the pumpkin and remove the fibres and seeds. Chop the flesh into small cubes.

2 Melt the butter in a saucepan. Stir in the pumpkin and brown lightly on all sides over medium heat. Sprinkle on the sugar and, when it has melted, add the milk, a little at a time.

3 Season with the ground mace and a little grated nutmeg and ground cloves, salt and pepper. Bring to the boil, then cover the pan and simmer the pumpkin over low heat for about 20 minutes.

4 Purée the soup in a blender or food processor, and return it to the pan. Bring back to the boil and adjust the seasoning, if necessary. Serve hot.

Variation:

Sweetcorn and pumpkin soup
Detach the kernels from 3 to 4 corn cobs (or use canned sweetcorn, drained). Mash or purée the kernels, and add them to the pumpkin in the above recipe. Pumpkin and sweetcorn were staple foods of the southwestern native Americans who often combined them in one dish.

Note: Pumpkin flesh freezes well. It can either be cut into cubes and blanched briefly in boiling water, or the pumpkin can be cooked through and then puréed before freezing.

Pumpkins

The best known of all the winter squashes, pumpkins are native to Central America, from where their cultivation spread northwards up the Mississippi valley thousands of years ago. They were brought to Europe in the late 16th century.

The delights of the pumpkin were passed by the native Americans to the early settlers, who soon learnt to appreciate this easy-to-grow vegetable, which not only kept well in the lean winter months but was rich in minerals and extremely versatile. Now grown all over the USA (as on the Vermont farm above), the sweet-flavoured flesh is made into soups, purées, cakes and the famous pumpkin pie. The seeds, when toasted, have a delicious nutty flavour.

Pumpkins can grow to 40 kilos or more, but smaller ones are generally more tender and succulent. Choose blemish-free pumpkins that feel heavy for their size. If buying a cut piece of pumpkin, check the flesh is firm.

Hollowed out pumpkin lanterns are part of the traditional American Hallowe'en festivities, when children in fancy dress go "trick or treating" from house to house asking for sweets and playing practical jokes.

Boston baked beans

Beans and pork with molasses served with brown bread　　　**Serves 6**

500 g small, dried, white haricot
beans
3 large onions
250 g rindless salt pork (or bacon,
if unavailable)
2 tbsp brown sugar
6 tbsp molasses
2 tsp dry mustard
1 tsp ground ginger
2 tbsp white wine vinegar
salt
freshly ground black pepper

For the bread:
70 g rye flour
70 g strong flour
70 g fine cornmeal
1 tbsp baking powder
½ tsp salt
4 tbsp molasses
¼ litre buttermilk
50 g seedless raisins (optional)

Preparation time: 45 minutes
(plus 12 hours' soaking time and
3 hours' cooking time)

2,700 kJ/640 calories per portion

1 Place the beans in a bowl and cover with water. Leave to soak overnight.

2 Drain the beans and put them in a saucepan with enough cold water to cover them. Bring to the boil and boil rapidly for 10 minutes, then drain in a sieve and rinse under running water.

3 Preheat the oven to 170°C (325°F or Mark 3). Peel the onions and chop into large pieces, then stir into the beans.

4 Cut the salt pork into 3 cm cubes. Spread half the meat over the base of a large ovenproof casserole. Cover with the beans and onions, and spread the rest of the meat on top.

5 Bring about ½ litre water to the boil in a saucepan. Add the brown sugar, molasses, mustard, ginger, vinegar, salt and pepper, and return to the boil, stirring constantly. Pour the mixture over the beans and stir lightly.

6 Cover the casserole and bake in the bottom of the oven for about 3 hours, until the beans are tender. Add more water from time to time, if the beans look like drying out.

7 As soon as the casserole is in the oven, stir all the ingredients for the bread to a smooth dough. Traditionally, the dough is baked in a well-greased food can. Alternatively, you can use a buttered, ¾ litre pudding basin or soufflé dish. Cover firmly with a sheet of greaseproof paper and foil tied on with string, or with a lid.

8 Fill a deep pan with water to a depth of about 4 cm. Place a trivet or steamer attachment in the pot, so that the can has no contact with the water. Bring to the boil, then stand the filled can or basin on the trivet, cover, and steam the bread for about 3 hours. Add a little more boiling water to the pan if too much evaporates during cooking.

9 Remove the bread from the can or basin while it is still hot. Slice it—this is traditionally done with stout string (*above*)—and serve with the beans.

Note: A similar version of this dish was cooked by the American Indians. It later became a tradition in Boston to serve it for supper on Saturday— baking day. The beans were baked in the oven with the bread in order to take advantage of the heat. If the family could afford it, the beans were enriched with boiled ham. Leftovers were served for breakfast the following morning, sometimes with eggs and bacon.

Boston brown bread was sometimes cooked in a *bain-mairie* in the same oven alongside the beans, but it has a better flavour and a lighter texture if it is steamed.

Cioppino

Fairly easy • San Francisco

Californian seafood soup

1 medium-sized onion
2 spring onions
1 small sweet green pepper
5 tbsp olive oil
1 garlic clove
400 g can peeled tomatoes
¼ litre dry red or white wine
30 g fresh parsley
2 sprigs fresh basil
2 sprigs fresh oregano
salt
freshly ground white pepper
about 400 g mixed fish fillets (for example, swordfish, tuna fish, sea bream, shark)
400 g live mussels or clams
200 g cooked, unpeeled deep sea prawns

Preparation time: 45 minutes

1,470 kJ/350 calories per portion

1 Peel the onion, wash and trim the spring onions, halve the sweet pepper lengthwise and remove the stalk, ribs and seeds. Finely chop all the vegetables. Heat the oil in a wide pan and stir-fry the chopped vegetables over medium heat for about 5 minutes.

2 Peel and crush the garlic and add to the pan. Add the tomatoes with their juice, followed by the wine. Mash the tomatoes with a spoon.

3 Wash and chop the herbs and add them to the pan. Season with salt and pepper, and simmer, uncovered, over low heat for about 10 minutes, stirring the mixture frequently.

4 Meanwhile, cut the fish into 3 cm cubes. Wash and scrub the mussels or clams very thoroughly under running water. Tap sharply any shells that are open and discard any that do not close.

5 Stir the fish and seafood into the other ingredients. Cover the pan and continue to simmer gently over low heat for about 5 to 8 minutes until the mussels open. Discard any that remain closed. Season the soup and serve hot.

Wine: A crisp white wine from the Napa Valley, California's most famous wine area, goes well with this soup.

Note: *Cioppino* was invented by Californian fishermen. Anything, depending on the day's catch, was thrown into the pot, and often cooked and eaten on the beach. You can vary this recipe with all kinds of different fish and shellfish.

Seafood gumbo

Creole fish stew

Fairly easy • Louisiana

2 medium-sized onions
3 sticks celery
1 sweet green pepper
4 tbsp vegetable oil
2 tbsp flour
4 garlic cloves
3 tbsp lemon juice
a few drops of Worcester sauce
a few drops of Tabasco sauce
1 tsp chopped fresh thyme
2 bay leaves
salt • freshly ground black pepper
300 g okra
3 spring onions • 15 g fresh parsley
200 g cooked, peeled prawns
75 g crab meat

Preparation time: 1½ hours

910 kJ/220 calories per portion

1 Peel the onions and wash and trim the celery, removing any tough strings. Halve the sweet pepper lengthwise and remove the stalk, ribs and seeds. Finely chop all the vegetables.

2 Heat the vegetable oil in a wide pan, add the flour and cook, stirring constantly, over high heat until dark brown. Do not let the flour turn black.

3 Add the chopped vegetables and stir thoroughly. Peel and crush the garlic, and add it to the vegetables in the pan.

4 Pour in ½ litre hot water and season with the lemon juice, Worcester sauce, Tabasco sauce, chopped thyme, bay leaves, salt and pepper. Cover and simmer the vegetables over low heat for about 30 minutes.

5 Meanwhile, wash and top and tail the okra. Cut it into thick slices and stir into the rest of the vegetables. Discard the bay leaves. Re-cover and simmer the gumbo over low heat for about 30 minutes.

6 Wash and trim the spring onions and cut them into thin rings. Wash the parsley, shake dry and chop finely. Add the spring onions, parsley, prawns and crab meat to the vegetables. Continue to simmer, covered, over low heat for a further 10 minutes. Taste and adjust the seasoning, if necessary. Serve on a bed of rice, if liked.

Note: If you prefer your vegetables crunchy and crisp, reduce the cooking time by about half.

Brunswick stew

Chicken and vegetable stew

Takes a little time • Virginia

Serves 4

1.5 kg oven-ready chicken
1 medium-sized onion
1 litre chicken stock
2 tomatoes
200 g floury potatoes
1 can sweetcorn (140 g drained
weight)
150 g frozen broad beans
15 g fresh parsley
salt • freshly ground black pepper
cayenne pepper

Preparation time: 1¼ hours

1,900 kJ/450 calories per portion

1 Wash the chicken in cold water, divide into large joints, and arrange in a large fireproof casserole or stockpot. Peel the onion, cut into rings and add to the chicken. Add the chicken stock, bring to the boil, cover and cook over medium heat for about 35 minutes.

2 Meanwhile, plunge the tomatoes into boiling water, skin them and remove the seeds, then finely chop the flesh. Peel the potatoes and cut into small dice. Remove the chicken joints from the casserole and set aside. Boil the stock, uncovered, over high heat until reduced to about ½ litre.

3 Drain the sweetcorn and add it to the stock together with the tomatoes, potatoes and beans. Simmer, covered, over low heat for about 15 minutes.

4 Meanwhile, remove the chicken meat from the bones and cut it into small pieces. Add the meat to the casserole and heat through briefly.

5 Wash the parsley, shake it dry and chop finely. Season the stew with salt, pepper and a little cayenne pepper. Sprinkle the chopped parsley over the top or stir it into the stew, then serve it piping hot.

Philadelphia pepper pot

Chunky veal, tripe and vegetable soup

Takes time • Philadelphia

Serves 6

1 kg knuckle of veal (ask the
butcher to saw or chop it)
400 g cleaned and blanched tripe
1 tsp black peppercorns
salt
1 large onion
2 sticks celery
1 small sweet red pepper
200 g floury potatoes
1 small, medium-hot, red chili
pepper (see Glossary)
50 g butter
3 tbsp flour
freshly ground black pepper
juice of ¼ lemon (optional)

**Preparation time: 45 minutes
(plus 2 hours' cooking time)**

1,200 kJ/290 calories per portion

1 Wash the veal and place in a large fireproof casserole or stockpot. Wash the tripe and add it to the veal.

2 Add 1½ litres water and bring it to the boil. Add the peppercorns and salt. Cover the casserole and simmer for about 1½ hours, or until the veal and the tripe are tender, then remove them from the cooking stock.

3 Bone the veal and cut it into small pieces. Cut the tripe into 1 cm-wide strips. Strain the stock through a fine sieve and reserve. Peel the onion. Trim and wash the celery. Halve the sweet pepper and remove the stalk, ribs and seeds. Finely chop all the vegetables.

4 Peel and wash the potatoes and cut them into small cubes. Slit open the chili pepper, remove the seeds, wash the chili and chop finely.

5 Melt the butter in a large saucepan and brown the onion, celery and pepper over low to medium heat until softened, stirring constantly.

6 Sprinkle the flour over the softened vegetables, stir until the flour turns golden, then slowly add the reserved stock. Simmer, uncovered, until the soup thickens slightly.

7 Add the potatoes, chili pepper, veal and tripe. Simmer over low heat for a further 30 minutes, with the casserole half covered by the lid. Season with salt, pepper and the lemon juice, if liked, and serve at once.

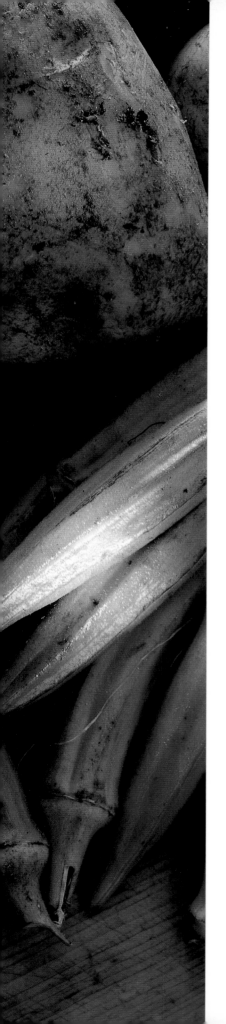

SIDE DISHES

Only a few of the vegetables in the vast cornucopia of fresh produce now enjoyed by Americans originated in North America. Of these the most important were maize, beans and pumpkins, which the native Americans taught early settlers how to cultivate and cook. They also showed them where to find mushrooms, wild rice and other edible wild plants.

Some vegetables such as tomatoes and sweet potatoes came from tropical America. Most others were brought in seed or tuber form by immigrants of many different nationalities, and in turn became part of the American diet. For example, German immigrants in the Northeast and Midwest introduced cabbage dishes such as sauerkraut, okra came from Africa with the slaves and Italians in California first planted artichokes—now a major industry.

Many of these vegetables are cooked in much the same way as in Europe. But there are also plenty of original New World recipes. The American Indian *succotash* (mixed sweetcorn and beans) was made from fresh vegetables in summer and dried ones in winter. Buttered boiled or baked corn on the cob is served as a simple side dish, as are corn oysters, which often accompany meat. Southerners like bean dishes such as Hoppin' John, served at New Year with glazed baked ham, or the Tex-Mex refried beans, served with grilled meat and tortillas. Relishes, pickles and chutneys are traditional accompaniments to meat.

Hoppin' John

Black-eyed beans and rice

Serves 4

**200 g dried black-eyed beans
(pinto or haricot beans can be used
instead)
250 g rindless, smoked lean streaky
bacon
1 large onion
1 tbsp vegetable oil
1 garlic clove
200 g long-grain rice
salt
freshly ground black pepper
a few drops of Tabasco sauce**

**Preparation time: 1¾ hours
(plus 12 hours' soaking time)**

2,700 kJ/640 calories per portion

1 Place the beans in a bowl and cover with water. Leave to soak overnight.

2 Drain the beans and put them in a saucepan with enough cold water to cover them. Bring to the boil and then continue to boil rapidly for 10 minutes. Then cover the pan and simmer over medium heat for about 1 hour.

3 Meanwhile, remove any gristle from the bacon and chop it into small dice. Peel and finely chop the onion.

4 Heat the oil in a frying pan and fry the bacon over medium heat until the fat runs. Add the chopped onion and fry until transparent. Peel and crush the garlic and add to the pan. Remove the pan from the heat.

5 Add the bacon and onion mixture and the rice to the beans, then cover and simmer over low heat for about 20 minutes, until the rice and beans are tender and the rice has absorbed the liquid. Add a little more boiling water if the mixture becomes too dry and starts to burn.

6 When cooked, season the mixture to taste with salt, pepper and Tabasco sauce, and serve hot.

Note: Hoppin' John is often served at New Year with glazed, baked ham and vegetables. Traditionally, a coin is hidden among the rice and beans, and whoever finds it can look forward to good fortune in the coming year.

Refried beans

Takes time • Texas

Fried cooked beans

Serves 6

250 g dried black or kidney beans
1 medium-sized onion
4 to 5 garlic cloves
2 beef tomatoes
45 g lard or 3 tbsp vegetable oil
salt
freshly ground black pepper
1 sprig fresh oregano
100 g soured cream (optional)

**Preparation time: 45 minutes
(plus 12 hours' soaking time and
about 2 hours' cooking time)**

890 kJ/210 calories per portion

1 Place the beans in a bowl and cover with water. Leave to soak overnight.

2 Drain the beans and put them in a saucepan with enough cold water to cover them. Bring to the boil and boil for 10 minutes, then cover and cook over low heat until tender. (According to the age and type of beans, this will take between 1½ to 2 hours.)

3 Drain the beans through a colander and reserve the cooking water. Peel and finely chop the onion and garlic. Wash the tomatoes, plunge them into boiling water, remove the skins and chop the flesh finely.

4 Heat the lard or oil gently in a large, heavy frying pan. It should not be too hot. Stir-fry the onion and garlic until transparent. Stir in the tomatoes.

5 Gradually add the cooked beans to the frying pan, mash them with a fork and fry briefly. Only add another batch of beans when the previous batch is slightly crisp at the edges.

6 When all the beans are used up, the mixture should be light and creamy. Stir in a little of the reserved cooking water to achieve this, if necessary.

7 Season the refried beans with salt and pepper. Strip the leaves from the oregano sprig and sprinkle the leaves over the beans. Serve, if liked, with soured cream, tortillas (*see Variation, page 118*) and salad.

Stuffed baked potatoes

Baked potatoes with a soured cream filling

Serves 4

4 large, equal-sized, waxy potatoes
2 tbsp vegetable oil
60 g butter
salt
freshly ground black pepper
125 g soured cream or crème fraîche
2 egg yolks

Preparation time: 45 minutes
(plus 1 hour's cooking time)

1,200 kJ/290 calories per portion

1 Preheat the oven to 200°C (400°F or Mark 6). Wash and scrub the potatoes thoroughly, prick them with a fork and brush them all over with the vegetable oil. Bake them on a grid in the centre of the oven for about 1 hour until soft.

2 Allow the cooked potatoes to cool a little, then cut a "lid" from the top of each one. Using a teaspoon, carefully scoop out the flesh, leaving shells about 1 cm thick (*above*).

3 Mash the scooped-out potato in a bowl with a fork. Stir in three quarters of the butter and let it melt slowly, then season the mashed potato to taste with salt and plenty of pepper.

4 Mix the soured cream and egg yolks together in a small bowl, then stir the mixture into the bowl of mashed potato. Season with a little more salt and pepper, if wished, and spoon the mixture back into the shells (*above*).

5 Arrange the potatoes side by side in a gratin dish. Flake the rest of the butter over the top of them (*above*) and then brown on the top shelf of the oven for a further 5 minutes.

Variation: Baked potato skins
These are a favourite snack in America. You need 5 small to medium-sized potatoes per person. Bake as described above, then halve the potatoes crosswise, scoop out the flesh and save it to use for some other dish. Sprinkle the potato halves with salt and pepper and arrange them side by side on a baking sheet. Sprinkle grated Cheddar cheese into each half, flake some butter on top and bake in the oven until the cheese has melted.

Note: Use really firm-fleshed waxy potatoes for this dish, to ensure the best possible flavour.

Candied sweet potatoes

Simple • New England

Sweet potatoes glazed with orange syrup

Serves 4

800 g sweet potatoes
salt
butter for the baking dish
100 g brown sugar
6 tbsp orange juice
50 g butter

Preparation time: 50 minutes

1,700 kJ/400 calories per portion

1 Wash the sweet potatoes and boil them, covered, in salted water over medium heat for about 10 minutes, until just cooked.

2 Drain the potatoes, leave to cool a little, then peel them. Preheat the oven to 180°C (350°F or Mark 4).

3 Butter a shallow baking dish. Cut the sweet potatoes into 1 to 2 cm-thick slices and arrange them in the dish so that they overlap.

4 Heat the sugar and orange juice in a small saucepan over low heat until the sugar has melted. Stir in the butter and leave it to melt.

5 Drizzle the warm orange syrup over the slices of sweet potato, then bake them in the centre of the oven for about 20 minutes.

Variation: Mashed sweet potatoes
This recipe also comes from New England. Boil 4 large sweet potatoes. Peel, then mash them. Stir in 30 to 45 g melted butter, 2 to 3 tbsp maple syrup and 1 tsp grated orange rind. Bake in the oven at 180°C (350°F or Mark 4) for about 25 minutes, until browned on top.

Note: Candied sweet potatoes are popular in many regions of the USA. In the Southern states, for example, a little whiskey and grated lemon rind is often stirred into the sugar syrup. Sometimes, chopped pecan nuts are sprinkled over the sweet potatoes just before they are baked in the oven.

Sweet potatoes

Sweet potatoes, also called batatas, are the large oblong or oval tubers of the convolvulous *Ipomoea batatas.* Native to tropical America, they are now cultivated in the southern United States as well as Central and South America, Asia and Africa. Often grown as a subsistence crop, they have a very high starch content and are among the foods regarded as vital to world economy.

With a sweetish taste, as its name suggests, the flesh of the sweet potato is either yellowish white or orange in colour with a pale brown or reddish skin. The orange variety is sometimes sold as yam (also in the USA), but yams, though similar, are less sweet and the two are not related.

Sweet potatoes can be boiled or baked in the same way as potatoes, and served as a vegetable or added to soups, casseroles, breads or puddings; they are best peeled after cooking. Americans serve candied sweet potatoes at Thanksgiving.

Corn on the cob

Fresh sweetcorn with butter   **Serves 4**

4 fresh corn on the cob
1 tbsp sugar
butter
salt
freshly ground black pepper

Preparation time: 20 minutes

290 kJ/69 calories per portion

1 Remove the green husks and silky threads from the corn cobs, if necessary, then rinse them under cold, running water.

2 Bring plenty of water (without any salt) to the boil in a large saucepan. Add the corn cobs and sugar to the boiling water. Cover the pan and cook the cobs over medium heat for about 8 minutes, until tender.

3 Lift the cobs out of the water with a slotted spoon or tongs. Drain, then top them with flakes of butter. Season with salt and pepper, and serve.

Note: The best way to test whether the corn is cooked is to stick the point of a sharp knife into the stalk end of the cob. The knife should slip in easily. Do not add salt to the cooking water as this may toughen the kernels. A little sugar in the water helps to bring out the sweetness of the corn.

Boiled corn on the cob is a favourite accompaniment to a variety of meat dishes in America. Often the corn is also grilled and brushed with spicy oil to give it a piquant flavour.

Corn oysters

Sweetcorn cakes   **Serves 4**

2 fresh corn on the cob
2 egg yolks
salt
freshly ground black pepper
freshly grated nutmeg
1 egg white
3 tbsp flour
clarified butter or oil for frying

Preparation time: 25 minutes

510 kJ/120 calories per portion

1 Remove the green husks and silky threads from the corn on the cob, if necessary, then rinse them under cold, running water. Detach the grains of corn from the cob with a sharp knife.

2 Mix the corn and the egg yolks in a bowl and season with salt, pepper and a little grated nutmeg.

3 Beat the egg white until stiff, then fold it into the corn mixture. Finally sprinkle the flour over the top and fold in loosely with a metal spoon.

4 Heat the clarified butter or oil in a large frying pan. Add the corn mixture, a tablespoonful at a time, to the hot fat, pressing down slightly with the spoon to form round cakes.

5 Fry the cakes over medium to high heat for about 2 minutes on each side, until they are golden-brown. Remove the cakes from the pan with a slotted spoon and drain thoroughly on paper towels. Serve immediately.

Note: You can buy fresh corn on the cob from around July to October. Look for plump, well-rounded cobs with tightly-packed, juicy kernels. If buying them in their husks, choose ones that are pale green with brown, silky tassels at the end. If fresh corn on the cob is unavailable, canned sweetcorn can be used for making corn oysters.

In the Great Plains they have a very similar recipe for corn fritters—small, flat cakes cooked in the frying pan.

Corn relish

Not difficult • All regions

Sweetcorn, pepper and cabbage relish

Makes three 40 cl jars

400 g white cabbage
1 large onion
1 sweet green pepper
1 sweet red pepper
2 cans sweetcorn (drained weight 285 g each)
150 g sugar
2 tsp salt
1 tsp dry mustard
freshly ground black pepper
½ litre cider vinegar

Preparation time: 1¾ hours

2,500 kJ/600 calories per jar

1 Trim, wash and shred the cabbage. Peel and finely chop the onion.

2 Halve, trim and wash the sweet red and green peppers, remove the ribs and seeds, then finely dice each half.

3 Drain the sweetcorn in a sieve, then place it in a wide saucepan with the prepared vegetables. Stir in the sugar, salt, mustard, a little pepper and the cider vinegar.

4 Bring the vinegar to the boil, then simmer the vegetables, uncovered, over low heat for about 1 hour, stirring frequently. Season the relish to taste, then transfer to warmed, clean jars while still hot and seal the jars with vinegar-proof lids immediately.

Variations: Relish can be made from other kinds of vegetables, and is often combined with fruit. In fact, any glut of produce in the summer can be made into a tasty relish.

Note: The above recipe will keep for about a year stored in a dark place. In America, corn relish is the essential relish to serve with steaks and other meat dishes. It is also a popular accompaniment to grills.

Cranberry sauce

Easy • New England

Traditional sauce to serve with turkey

Serves 8 to 10

200 g cranberries
100 g brown sugar
500 g tart apples
1 to 2 tsp grated rind of an unwaxed orange
ground cloves

Preparation time: 30 minutes

310 kJ/74 calories per portion (if serving 10)

1 Wash and sort the cranberries, mix them with the brown sugar in a wide saucepan and add 12.5 cl water.

2 Peel, quarter and core the apples. Slice crosswise and add immediately to the cranberries in the pan.

3 Cover the pan and simmer the fruit over low heat for about 15 minutes, stirring from time to time, and adding more water if the fruit becomes too dry. Season the sauce with the grated orange rind and a little ground cloves.

4 Pour into a bowl, cover, and store in the refrigerator until ready to use.

Note: Cranberry sauce is one of the classic accompaniments to roast turkey at Thanksgiving (*recipe, page 98*). As with all classic recipes, there are many variations. It is sometimes made with oranges, sometimes without the apples, and occasionally with rather more spice.

In New England, cranberry sauce is also a traditional accompaniment to serve with pot-roast beef.

Fried green tomatoes
Deep-fried tomato slices

Simple • The South

Serves 4

6 green or pale red tomatoes
(see Note)
75 g plain flour
75 g cornmeal
1 tbsp brown sugar
salt
freshly ground black pepper
1 litre oil for deep-frying

Preparation time: 20 minutes

2,100 kJ/500 calories per portion

1 Wash and dry the tomatoes and cut them into 5 mm to 1 cm-thick slices.

2 Mix the flour and cornmeal with the sugar, salt and pepper on a plate or in a shallow dish. Coat the tomato slices in the mixture, shaking off any excess.

3 Heat the oil in a heavy pan until bubbles rise from a wooden chopstick dipped in the oil. If you are using an electric deep fryer, preheat to 180°C (350°F). Fry the tomatoes in batches until golden-brown on both sides.

4 Remove the cooked slices from the pan with a slotted spoon, and place them briefly on paper towels to drain off some of the cooking fat.

Variation: Fried onion rings
Onions can be prepared in the same way as the tomatoes. Peel 300 g medium-sized onions and cut them into rings. Dip them in the flour mixture and fry until golden-brown.

Note: American cooks use really green, unripe tomatoes for this recipe. These contain tomatine, which is similar to solanine in potatoes (the green patches). High amounts of either of these natural plant chemicals can cause stomach upsets—a normal-sized portion of green tomatoes should cause no problems. The chemical disappears as the tomato ripens.
  Fried green tomatoes go well with fish and meat dishes.

Succotash
Beans and sweetcorn

Quick • New England

Serves 4

1 small onion
30 g butter
1 can sweetcorn (drained weight
285 g, with the liquid reserved)
1 can lima or butter beans
(drained weight about 330 g, with
the liquid reserved)
2 sprigs fresh parsley
salt
freshly ground white pepper
2 to 3 tbsp soured cream

Preparation time: 20 minutes

1,500 kJ/360 calories per portion

1 Peel and finely chop the onion. Heat the butter in a saucepan and fry the onion until transparent.

2 Stir in the canned sweetcorn and the beans, each with their reserved liquid, and cook the mixture over low heat for 10 minutes, stirring occasionally.

3 Wash the parsley, shake it dry and chop finely. Season the vegetables with salt and pepper.

4 Finally, stir in the soured cream and the chopped parsley, and serve.

Note: This is one of the USA's oldest vegetable dishes, inherited by the early settlers from the Indians. In summer it is made with fresh ingredients, while in winter dry or canned ones are used.
  Succotash is often served as a side dish with ham baked with a honey and spicy glaze. To make the glaze, mix together 150 g honey, a little pepper and paprika, and 20 cl water. Rub a 1.25 kg ham with the glaze and bake in the centre of the oven at 200°C (400°F or Mark 6) for about 1 hour, brushing the ham with the glaze from time to time during the cooking.

FISH AND SEAFOOD

E ndless coastlines, great lakes and countless rivers have long provided Americans with an abundance of fish and shellfish. Though pollution and overfishing have taken their toll, fish farms and the reintroduction of fish into rivers and lakes has helped to boost numbers.

Pacific and Atlantic fish differ, and freshwater fish also vary depending on climate and terrain, so every region has its own specialities. For example, pompano, red snapper and swordfish live in the Atlantic, whereas the king salmon and certain flounders are found in the northwest Pacific. Similarly, there are different varieties of clams, lobsters and oysters. Crabs range from the West Coast Dungeness to Florida's stone crabs, and the blue and softshell crabs of Virginia and the Carolinas.

Maine is famous for its lobsters and mussels, and Atlantic cod is popular on the northeast coast. Freshwater crayfish (called crawfish in America) and prawns abound in Louisiana and are included in many Creole and Cajun dishes, such as jambalaya.

Americans have always liked to cook fish in the open, whether at a New England clambake, grilling trout over a campfire or a Californian *cioppino* cooked on the beach, using fish and shellfish straight out of the ocean. The important thing to remember is that the fresher the fish, the better it tastes, and overcooking will dry out the delicate flesh and make it tough.

Lobster Newburg

Lobster in rich creamy sauce

More complex • New York

Serves 4

2 fresh lobsters (about 800 g each)
or 2 cooked lobsters
2 shallots
60 g butter
1 tsp flour
4 tbsp dry Madeira or sherry
20 cl single cream
2 egg yolks
salt
cayenne pepper

Preparation time: 1 hour

2,600 kJ/620 calories per portion

1 Bring plenty of water to the boil in a large saucepan. Grasp one lobster by the back and plunge it head first into the boiling water. Cover the pan with a lid, weighing down the lid for the first 2 minutes. Simmer gently for about 15 minutes, then lift out and repeat the procedure with the second lobster.

2 With your left hand, hold one lobster firmly around the breastplate and twist the claws away from the body.

3 Take the lobster in both hands and bend the tail upwards or downwards until it breaks off (*above*).

4 Using both thumbs, prise out the tail meat (*above*). Remove and discard the dark, vein-like intestine, the stomach (which is located near the head) and the spongy gills. Repeat the procedure with the second lobster.

5 Remove the small lower pincers and gristle. Twist off the lower joint. Pull this joint apart (*above*) and remove the meat. Up-end the large piece of the claws on the work surface and strike the thick end hard with a knife to split it. Carefully pull the meat out of the claws and chop it into dice or leave the pieces whole.

6 Peel the shallots and very finely chop them. Melt the butter in a wide pan and fry the shallots over low heat until transparent. Sprinkle the flour over them and brown lightly, then add the Madeira or sherry, a little at a time, stirring constantly. Stir in the cream. Simmer for about 4 minutes, while continuing to stir.

7 Pour a little of the sauce into a cup or bowl and whisk in the egg yolks. Return the mixture to the pan and add the lobster meat. Heat through for a few minutes until the sauce thickens. Do not allow the sauce to come to the boil, otherwise it may curdle.

8 Season the sauce to taste with salt and cayenne pepper. Serve the lobster and creamy sauce with slices of toast or on a bed of boiled rice.

Crab cakes

Not difficult • Maryland

Fried crab cakes with yogurt sauce

Serves 4

1 egg • 15 g flat-leaf parsley
2 shallots • 2 tbsp mayonnaise
½ tsp medium-hot made mustard
salt • cayenne pepper
75 g bread from a white tin loaf
5 tbsp milk
400 g canned crab meat
1 lemon
vegetable oil for frying

For the sauce:
2 shallots • 10 g chives
15 g parsley • 1 tbsp capers
1 gherkin • 150 g mayonnaise
100 g whole milk yogurt
1 tsp dry mustard
salt • cayenne pepper

Preparation time: 30 minutes
(plus 1 hour's chilling time)

1,200 kJ/290 calories per portion

1 Break the egg into a bowl. Wash the parsley and shake dry. Peel the shallots. Chop both very finely and mix with the egg, mayonnaise and mustard. Season with salt and cayenne pepper, and mix thoroughly.

2 Remove the bread crusts, then tear the bread into pieces and place it in a small bowl. Drizzle the milk over it.

3 Finely chop the crab meat and add it to the parsley mixture with the soaked bread. Mix thoroughly.

4 Shape the mixture into eight small, round cakes. Arrange the cakes on a chopping board, cover with a piece of greaseproof paper and leave to chill in the refrigerator for about 1 hour.

5 Meanwhile, make the sauce. Peel the shallots. Wash the chives and the parsley, and shake dry. Finely chop the shallots, herbs, capers and gherkin.

6 Mix all the chopped ingredients with the mayonnaise, yogurt and mustard. Season with salt and cayenne pepper.

7 Wash and dry the lemon, and cut it into eight wedges. Heat plenty of oil in a deep frying pan and fry the crab cakes, in batches, for 2 to 3 minutes on each side, until golden-brown.

8 Drain the cooked crab cakes on paper towels. Serve garnished with the lemon wedges and accompanied by the cold yogurt sauce.

Jambalaya

Not difficult • New Orleans

Rice with prawns, vegetables and ham

Serves 4

salt
200 g round-grain rice
2 medium-sized onions
1 garlic clove
2 fresh hot chili peppers (see Glossary)
3 sticks celery
1 sweet pepper
30 g fresh parsley
45 g butter
1 small can peeled tomatoes
1 tbsp tomato purée
ground cloves
cayenne pepper
freshly ground black pepper
200 g cooked ham (in a thick slice)
250 g peeled, cooked, deep-sea prawns

Preparation time: 45 minutes

1,900 kJ/450 calories per portion

1 Bring about 60 cl lightly salted water to the boil in a saucepan. Trickle the rice into the pan, cover and cook over low heat for about 20 minutes.

2 Meanwhile, peel and finely chop the onions. Peel and chop the garlic. Slit the chili peppers open, remove the seeds, wash the chili peppers and cut them into thin rings.

3 Wash, trim and thinly slice the celery, removing any tough strings. Halve the pepper, remove the stalk, ribs and seeds, then wash and cut into thin strips. Wash the parsley, shake it dry and finely chop the leaves.

4 Heat the butter in a large saucepan until it froths, then fry the onions over medium heat until transparent. Add the garlic, chili peppers, celery and sweet pepper. Stir-fry the vegetables for about 5 minutes.

5 Add the tomatoes with their juice and crush them slightly with a large wooden spoon.

6 Stir in the tomato purée and half the chopped parsley, and season to taste with a little ground cloves, cayenne pepper, salt and black pepper. Simmer over low heat for about 5 minutes.

7 Meanwhile, drain the rice through a sieve. Cut the ham into 1 cm dice. Place the prawns in a colander and rinse under cold running water.

8 Stir the rice, ham and prawns into the tomato sauce. Heat through for about 5 minutes, then adjust the seasoning and serve, sprinkled with the rest of the chopped parsley.

Creamed scallops

Scallops in an anise-flavoured mushroom and cream sauce

Not difficult · The South

Serves 4

250 g button mushrooms
1 small sweet red pepper
2 spring onions
60 g butter
20 cl double cream
1 tbsp anise-flavoured liqueur (such as anisette)
salt
freshly ground white pepper
12 shelled scallops (about 450 g)

Preparation time: 30 minutes

1,800 kJ/430 calories per portion

1 Wash, trim and slice the button mushrooms. Halve the pepper and remove the ribs and seeds, then wash it and cut into thin strips. Wash and trim the spring onions and cut them into thin rings.

2 Melt the butter in a wide pan and stir-fry all the prepared vegetables for about 5 minutes, until softened.

3 Stir the cream and anise-flavoured liqueur into the vegetable mixture, and season to taste with salt and pepper.

4 Wash and dry the scallops, cut in half, if necessary, and add them to the pan. Heat through over very low heat for about 5 minutes. Serve the scallops with boiled rice.

Variation: Grilled scallops

In New England, scallops are also marinated and then grilled on skewers. Make a marinade from a finely chopped onion, 6 tbsp lemon juice, salt and a little white pepper. Marinate the scallops for 1 to 2 hours, then thread them onto long skewers and cook over charcoal or under a preheated grill for 8 to 10 minutes, brushing them from time to time with a little melted butter.

Note: Some cooks thicken the cream sauce either with a little cornflour, dissolved in water, stirred into the sauce, or with a beaten egg yolk.

Scallops

Scallops are bivalve molluscs with beautiful fluted, fan-shaped shells, which are often used as containers in which to serve them. Along America's east coast, dragnets gather sea scallops and the much-prized bay scallops off the seabed, while the catch on the west coast consists of Pacific scallops. Winter is the scallop season.

The firm, succulent flesh should look fresh, with a sweet smell and moist sheen. When buying, make sure the shells are firmly shut, but if you are unused to preparing them, you can buy fresh scallops prepared on the shell. Frozen ones usually come shelled, often without their corals.

The entire scallop can be eaten, including the coral—or roe—but, though Europeans consider the coral a delicacy, Americans seldom eat it. Scallops can be poached, deep-fried, grilled on skewers, sautéed in butter or served in a sauce in their shells, in the French manner.

Blackened fish

Spicy fish cooked on a barbecue

Fairly easy • Louisiana

Serves 4

4 fish fillets (for example, red snapper) each about 150 g, no more than 2 cm thick and preferably of even thickness
2 sprigs fresh basil
1 small onion
1 garlic clove
1 tbsp sweet paprika
1 tsp salt
1 tsp cayenne pepper
1 tsp citric pepper
1 tsp dried thyme
50 g butter
6 tbsp olive oil
lemon wedges and parsley for garnish (optional)

Preparation time: 30 minutes

1,300 kJ/310 calories per portion

1 Preheat the barbecue (*see Note*). Wash and dry the fish fillets.

2 To make the spice mixture, wash the basil, shake dry and chop finely. Peel and very finely chop the onion and the garlic. Mix on a plate with the paprika, salt, cayenne pepper, citric pepper and dried thyme.

3 Heat a heavy, cast-iron frying pan over the barbecue coals until very hot. Meanwhile, melt the butter in a small saucepan, pour it on to a soup plate and stir in the olive oil.

4 Dip the fish fillets first in the butter and oil, then coat them in the spice mixture. Lay them in the hot frying pan and fry for 1 to 2 minutes only on each side. Take care, they may spit! Garnish with the lemon wedges and parsley, if using. Serve with salad and boiled rice or potatoes.

Variation: Other fish that can be cooked in this way are redfish, catfish and pompano. Chicken joints can be "blackened", too.

Note: In America blackened fish is always cooked outdoors in a cast-iron frying pan over a glowing-hot barbecue. Indoors, there would be too much smoke. However, if you do want to cook the fish in your kitchen, open the windows wide and turn on the extractor fan, if you have one.

Catfish with hush puppies

Fairly easy • The South   **Fried catfish with cornmeal dumplings**   *Serves 4*

For the hush puppies:
1 medium-sized onion
150 fine cornmeal
2 tbsp wholewheat flour
1 tbsp cornflour
1 tsp baking powder • 1 tsp salt
1 egg • 12.5 cl lukewarm milk
vegetable oil for deep-frying

For the catfish:
500 g catfish • 3 tbsp fine cornmeal
2 tbsp wholewheat flour
salt • freshly ground white pepper
cayenne pepper
vegetable oil for frying
1 unwaxed lemon
lettuce leaves for garnish
bottled chili sauce, to serve

Preparation time: 40 minutes

2,200 kJ/520 calories per portion

1 To make the hush puppies, peel and very finely chop the onion. Mix with the cornmeal, flours, baking powder, salt, egg and milk to a not-too-firm dough.

2 Divide the catfish into portion-sized pieces. Mix the cornmeal, flour, salt, white pepper and cayenne pepper on a plate. Dip the catfish pieces in the mixture until thoroughly coated.

3 Heat the oil for deep-frying the hush puppies in a heavy pan until bubbles rise from a wooden chopstick dipped in the oil. If using an electric deep fryer, preheat to 180°C (350°F).

4 Spoon the dough into the hot oil, a tablespoonful at a time, dipping the spoon right into the oil. Fry the hush puppies for 2 to 3 minutes, turning them as they cook. Remove from the

pan with a slotted spoon and drain them well on paper towels.

5 Meanwhile, heat the oil for the fish in a wide frying pan. Place the fish in the pan and fry over medium heat for 3 to 4 minutes on each side, until they are golden-brown.

6 Wash and dry the lemon and lettuce. Cut the lemon into eight wedges. Serve the catfish and hush puppies together, garnished with the lemon and lettuce, and accompanied by chili sauce.

Note: There is an amusing story attached to the unusual name of "hush puppies". In the old days, so the story goes, the fishermen used to cook their catch on the river bank, and in order to keep the barking dogs quiet, some of the flour coating for the fish was rolled into little balls and thrown to the dogs with a cry of: "Hush, puppies".

Salt cod balls

Deep-fried salt cod and potato balls

Serves 4

500 g dried salt cod
500 g floury potatoes
salt
60 g butter, softened
2 egg yolks
1 tsp dry mustard
Worcester sauce
freshly ground white pepper
1 to 2 tbsp fresh breadcrumbs
(optional)
1 litre vegetable oil for deep-frying

Preparation time: 50 minutes
(plus 12 hours' soaking time)

3,500 kJ/830 calories per portion

1 Lay the fish in a bowl and cover with cold water. Cover the bowl and leave the fish to soak in the refrigerator for at least 12 hours, changing the water three or four times.

2 When you are ready to cook, rinse the salt cod under cold running water, place it in a saucepan and add enough water to reach 1 to 2 cm above the fish. Bring the water to the boil, then reduce the heat and gently simmer the fish over low heat, with the lid half covering the saucepan, for 20 minutes, until the flesh is tender.

3 Drain the fish, then carefully remove all the bones and skin (*above*). Break the flesh into small pieces with a fork.

4 Meanwhile, peel the potatoes, cut them into chunks, and cook in lightly salted water over medium heat for 20 to 30 minutes, until tender. Drain the potatoes and while still hot, mash finely or pass through a potato ricer into a large bowl.

5 Blend the mashed potatoes with the fish, butter and egg yolks, then season with the mustard, Worcester sauce and pepper. If the dough is too soft, add 1 to 2 tbsp breadcrumbs, or a little flour.

6 Heat the oil in a large heavy pan until bubbles rise from a wooden chopstick dipped in the oil. If using an electric deep fryer, preheat to 180°C (350°F). Cook the salt cod balls in small batches, adding the potato and fish dough to the fat, a tablespoonful at a time (*above*). Fry the fish balls for about 4 minutes, until golden-brown.

7 Remove the cooked fish balls from the pan with a slotted spoon and drain thoroughly on paper towels (*above*). Serve, if liked, with coleslaw (*recipe, page 40*) or Boston baked beans (*recipe, page 60*).

Note: Cape Cod, where the Pilgrim Fathers landed in America, takes its name from the fish, which the settlers ate fresh in summer and dried during the winter months.

Americans eat the leftover salt cod balls for breakfast the following day, accompanied by brown bread.

Steamed salmon steaks

Fairly easy · Oregon **Steamed salmon with a dill-flavoured cream sauce** *Serves 4*

1 small onion
1 leek
1 stick celery
1 bay leaf
12.5 cl dry white wine
40 cl fish stock
salt
freshly ground black pepper
1 small, unwaxed lemon
4 salmon steaks (about 250 g each)
2 tbsp butter
2 tbsp flour
10 cl double cream
15 g fresh dill

Preparation time: 35 minutes

2,700 kJ/640 calories per portion

1 Peel the onion, wash and trim the leek and celery, and coarsely chop all the vegetables. Place them in a wide pan with the bay leaf, white wine and fish stock. Season the steaming liquid with salt and pepper.

2 Wash the lemon, cut it into eight wedges and add to the pan. Bring the liquid in the pan to the boil.

3 Wash the salmon steaks and lay them side by side in a steamer. Place the steamer in the pan, cover tightly and steam the fish over medium heat for 8 to 12 minutes (according to the thickness of the fillets).

4 Meanwhile, melt the butter in a saucepan. Add the flour and fry until golden, stirring constantly. Add the cream and simmer over low heat.

5 When the salmon steaks are cooked, transfer them to a serving dish and keep warm. Strain about 20 cl of the stock through a fine sieve into the cream sauce and heat through. Season with salt and pepper, if necessary.

6 Wash the dill, shake it dry and chop finely, then stir it into the sauce. Serve the salmon steaks with the sauce, accompanied, if liked, by lightly steamed vegetables.

Note: Salmon is also good served with other creamy sauces, such as sauce mousseline (hollandaise sauce with whipped cream).

Fish with orange

Simple · Florida **Fish cooked in an orange marinade** *Serves 4*

1 large unwaxed orange
1 medium-sized onion
1 tsp salt
4 fish fillets (about 200 g each · see Note)
freshly grated nutmeg
freshly ground black pepper
thinly sliced orange and some orange rind cut into matchsticks for garnish (optional)

Preparation time: 25 minutes (plus 30 minutes' marinating time)

690 kJ/160 calories per portion

1 Wash and dry the orange. Grate off a little rind, then halve the orange and squeeze out the juice.

2 Peel and finely chop the onion. Put it in a wide bowl with the orange juice and rind, and the salt.

3 Rinse the fish fillets in cold water, pat them dry and place in the orange marinade. Turn the fish to coat it with the marinade, then cover the bowl and leave to stand at room temperature for about 30 minutes.

4 After about 15 minutes, preheat the oven to 200°C (400°F or Mark 6).

5 Arrange the fish fillets side by side in a gratin dish, then sprinkle lightly with grated nutmeg and pepper.

6 Bake in the centre of the oven for about 10 minutes, basting frequently with the orange marinade. If you like, garnish with sliced orange and orange rind matchsticks. Serve immediately with boiled rice.

Note: In Florida, pompano and red snapper are usually used for this dish. Both are saltwater fish with very delicate, white flesh. You can also use other types, such as bass, monkfish or cod (which is cheaper).

Stuffed trout

Trout stuffed with spinach and bacon

Fairly easy • Rocky Mountains

Serves 4

400 g leaf spinach
4 trout (about 300 g each)
salt
freshly ground black pepper
1 medium-sized onion
100 g bacon in thin rashers
3 tbsp fresh breadcrumbs
12.5 cl double cream
30 g butter, plus a little extra for
greasing the dish
lemon wedges for garnish
(optional)

**Preparation time: 30 minutes
(plus 30 minutes' cooking time)**

2,900 kJ/690 calories per portion

1 Carefully wash and sort the spinach, discarding withered leaves and tough stalks. Place the spinach in a wide pan with just the water that clings to the leaves, cover the pan and cook over medium heat for about 4 minutes, until the spinach wilts. Drain the spinach, squeeze out as much water as possible and chop very finely.

2 Thoroughly wash and clean the trout and pat them dry with paper towels. Sprinkle the fish inside and out with salt and pepper (*above*). Peel and finely chop the onion.

3 Fry the bacon rashers in a wide pan over medium heat until crisp, then lay them on paper towels and pat to remove the surplus fat. Fry the chopped onion in the fat in the pan until transparent.

4 Chop or crumble the bacon rashers and add to the spinach, together with the fried onion. Add the breadcrumbs and double cream, and stir thoroughly to combine the ingredients. Season with pepper and a little salt. Preheat the oven to 180°C (350°F or Mark 4).

5 Using a tablespoon, spoon some of the bacon and spinach stuffing into each trout (*above*) then lay the fish side by side in a greased baking dish.

6 Flake the butter over the top of the fish (*above*). Cover the dish with a lid and bake in the centre of the oven for about 30 minutes. Remove the fish from the dish and serve garnished with lemon wedges, if wished.

Variation: An alternative stuffing can be made with 8 finely chopped, medium-sized, cooked prawns stirred into a thick, creamy béchamel sauce.

Note: Wild trout frolic in America's mountain streams and there are also many fish farms, especially in Idaho, where they breed rainbow trout in large numbers. They are a favourite fish with cooks and are often served on a bed of pine or fir twigs.

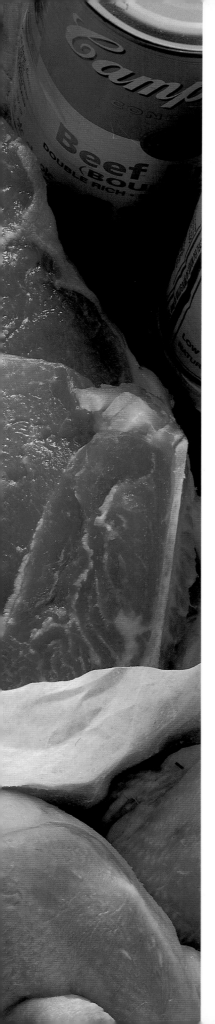

MEAT AND POULTRY

Beef is America's favourite meat, followed by pork or ham and chicken. Lamb and veal tend to feature less often on the menu.

Things were very different in the 17th century, before cattle grazed the prairies and the railway networks made transportation easier. Native Americans hunted bison and game birds, and the Pilgrim Fathers might not have survived without wildfowl such as turkeys—which is why roast turkey was the focal point of their first Thanksgiving feast.

The settlers also hunted quail, geese, ducks, larks, pigeons and partridges, which they roasted over an open fire or cooked into stews in huge iron pots. Later, as the wagons rolled westwards, the pioneers found bison, antelopes or bears, mountain sheep, elk, deer, hares, raccoons and squirrels.

Although hunting is still a favourite sport, wildlife is less plentiful and many species are protected, so game has become more of a delicacy; however, quail and wild turkey are now farmed.

Cattle from gigantic grazing herds in Texas and the western ranges (or fed on maize and soybeans on intensive Midwest farms) supply prime cuts for grilling: tender fillets, rib steaks, top sirloin and huge T-bone or porterhouse steaks. Other cuts are turned into hamburgers or dishes such as New England boiled dinner and chili con carne. Pork favourites included barbecued spareribs, while Southern fried chicken and chicken à la king are just two of countless chicken recipes.

Thanksgiving Day turkey

Roast turkey stuffed with corn bread

Serves 8 to 10

For the corn bread:
100 g plain flour
100 g fine cornmeal
1 tsp baking powder
1 tbsp sugar • ½ tsp salt
4 tbsp vegetable oil
100 g soured cream
10 cl milk • 1 egg

For the turkey:
1 onion • 2 sticks celery
75 g butter • 200 g sausage meat
30 g parsley • 4 sprigs fresh thyme
3 sprigs fresh sage
salt • freshly ground black pepper
20 cl chicken stock
3.5 kg oven-ready turkey
45 g clarified butter

For the gravy:
40 cl chicken stock
30 g butter • 2 tbsp flour
a little cream (optional)

*Preparation time: 1¼ hours
(plus 25 minutes' baking time and
2 hours' roasting time, and up to 2
days' resting time for the bread)*

*3,300 kJ/790 calories per portion
(if serving 10)*

1 Bake the bread a day or two before the meal. Preheat the oven to 200°C (400°F or Mark 6). Thoroughly grease an 18 cm square baking tin with a little oil. Working fast, mix all the bread ingredients thoroughly in a bowl. Transfer the dough to the baking tin and bake on the bottom shelf of the oven for about 25 minutes.

2 On the day of the meal, peel and finely chop the onion, wash and finely chop the celery. Heat the butter in a frying pan until frothy, then fry the onion and celery over low heat for about 5 minutes. Add the sausage meat and fry for a further 3 to 4 minutes, stirring constantly.

3 Wash the parsley, thyme and sage, shake dry and chop finely. Stir them into the sausage meat and vegetable mixture. Season with salt and pepper.

4 Cut the corn bread into 3 cm cubes and stir them into the sausage meat mixture a little at a time, together with the stock. The mixture should be moist but not sloppy. You may not need to use all the corn bread as the quantity given is quite generous.

5 Wash the turkey and pat dry with paper towels. Rub it inside and out with salt and pepper, and stuff with the corn bread stuffing. Sew up the body cavity with kitchen twine and truss the bird— twisting the wings behind the back and binding the legs together—so that it keeps its shape and cooks evenly.

6 Preheat the oven to 180°C (350°F or Mark 4). Heat the clarified butter in a large roasting pan on the top of the stove, then brown the turkey on all sides over high heat. When browned, turn it breast down in the pan and place it on the bottom shelf in the oven.

7 Roast the turkey for at least 2 hours, turning it as it browns and basting it with the pan juices from time to time. To test whether the turkey is cooked, pierce the thickest part of the thigh with a fine skewer. If the meat juices run clear, the turkey is ready. Transfer the turkey to a meat dish.

8 Turn off the oven and return the turkey to the oven to keep warm while you make the gravy. First, skim the clear layer of fat from the surface of the pan juices with a spoon and mop up any remaining fat with paper towels. Add the stock to the pan juices and stir well to scrap up any particles stuck to the bottom of the pan. Pour the gravy into a saucepan and bring to the boil.

9 Knead the butter and flour together, then stir a small knob at a time into the gravy. Bring to the boil over high heat until it thickens, then adjust the seasoning. If you like, stir in a little cream. Serve with the turkey.

Accompaniments: Cranberry sauce (*recipe, page 77*) and candied sweet potatoes (*recipe, page 72*) are served with the Thanksgiving turkey. Mashed potatoes, sweetcorn, wild rice or broccoli are also popular side dishes.

Variation: Instead of corn bread, you can use day-old wheat bread for the stuffing. You will need about 4 thick slices from a tin loaf. If all the stuffing does not fit in the turkey, you can place the rest in an ovenproof dish and bake for the last 15 minutes of the turkey cooking time, then serve it separately.

Note: Stuffed turkey is probably the most traditional and widely used dish in the whole of the United States and is served throughout the nation on Thanksgiving Day.

Southern fried chicken

Fried marinated chicken joints

Quick • The South

Serves 4

1.8 kg oven-ready chicken
salt
freshly ground black pepper
milk
vegetable oil for deep frying
flour

Preparation time: 30 minutes

2,500 kJ/600 calories per portion

1 Divide the chicken into eight joints. Wash and dry the joints, then rub all over with salt and pepper. Place them in a deep bowl and cover with milk, then leave them to stand for at least 15 minutes. Meanwhile, preheat the oven to its minimum setting.

2 Heat the oil in a heavy pan, until bubbles rise from a wooden chopstick dipped in the hot oil. If you are using an electric deep fryer, preheat to 180°C (350°F). Remove the chicken from the milk, pat dry and sprinkle all over with flour. Fry the joints in batches in the oil for about 10 minutes, until golden-brown, then remove from the pan.

3 Keep cooked chicken joints warm in the oven while cooking the remainder. Serve as soon as they are all cooked.

Variation: Chicken royal

Southern fried chicken served with vegetables and a creamy béchamel sauce is known as chicken royal. To make the sauce, melt 30 g butter in a pan, sprinkle in 2 tbsp flour and stir the roux over medium heat until golden. Stir in 20 cl chicken stock and 10 cl cream, and cook for a few minutes until the sauce is thick and creamy. Season with salt and pepper.

Chicken à la king

Chicken in a rich creamy sauce

Fairly easy • New York

Serves 4

1.5 kg oven-ready chicken
1 tbsp peppercorns
2 bay leaves
1 small sweet green pepper
200 g button mushrooms
60 g butter
2 tbsp flour
20 cl double cream
salt
freshly ground white pepper
sweet paprika
2 egg yolks
1 small, medium-hot red chili pepper (see Glossary)
2 to 3 tbsp dry sherry

Preparation time: 1½ hours

2,800 kJ/670 calories per portion

1 Wash the chicken and place it in a large saucepan with just enough cold water to cover it. Add the peppercorns and bay leaves. Bring the water to the boil, then half cover the pan with the lid and simmer the chicken over medium heat for about 45 minutes.

2 Lift the chicken out of the cooking stock, discard the skin and bones, and cut the meat into strips. Strain the stock and reserve about 30 cl.

3 Wash the sweet pepper and remove the stalk, ribs and seeds, then cut into shreds. Wash and thinly slice the mushrooms. Melt the butter in a saucepan, add the vegetables and stir-fry over low heat for about 5 minutes.

4 Sprinkle the flour over the top of the vegetables, continue to fry briefly, then gradually stir in the reserved stock, followed by the cream. Bring to the boil and season with salt, pepper and paprika. Simmer for about 6 minutes, then add the chicken and heat through.

5 Pour a little sauce from the pan into a bowl and stir in the egg yolks. Return the mixture to the pan. Heat through briefly, but do not allow it to boil.

6 Slit open the chili pepper, remove the seeds, wash it and cut into very thin rings. Stir the chili rings and sherry into the chicken and season well with salt and pepper. Serve, sprinkled with a little paprika, if liked.

Stuffed quail
Quail stuffed with wild rice

Serves 4

1 medium-sized onion
30 g butter
125 g wild rice
¼ litre chicken stock
8 oven-ready quail
salt
freshly ground black pepper
8 thin rashers smoked bacon
60 g melted butter for basting

For the sauce:
200 g small button mushrooms
1 medium-sized onion
2 tbsp flour
¼ litre chicken stock
2 sprigs fresh thyme
2 tbsp whiskey
salt
freshly ground black pepper
2 tbsp double cream

Preparation time: 1¾ hours

3,300 kJ/790 calories per portion

1 To make the stuffing, peel and finely chop the onion. Melt the butter in a large saucepan and fry the onion over low heat until transparent. Add the wild rice and stock, bring to the boil, then cover and cook over low heat for 20 to 45 minutes, until the rice is tender.

2 Meanwhile, preheat the oven to 200°C (400°F or Mark 6). Rub the quail with salt and pepper.

3 Drain the wild rice through a sieve, season with salt and pepper and then loosely stuff the quail with it. Sew up the body cavities with kitchen twine.

4 Lay the quail side by side, breast up, in an ungreased roasting pan. Place a loosely folded rasher of bacon over each bird. Roast in the centre of the oven for about 20 minutes, basting frequently with melted butter and the juices from the roasting pan.

5 To make the sauce, trim and thinly slice the mushrooms. Peel and finely chop the onion. Remove the quail from the oven and turn off the heat. Transfer the quail and bacon to a serving dish and keep warm in the oven.

6 Add the mushrooms and onion to the roasting pan. Cook on the hob over medium heat for a few minutes, stirring constantly. Sprinkle the flour over the vegetables. Add the stock. Cook until the sauce becomes thick and creamy.

7 Wash the thyme, shake it dry and chop finely. Stir it into the sauce with the whiskey and season with salt and pepper. Add the cream, then serve the sauce with the quail.

Wild rice

Wild rice, or Indian rice, with its long, thin black grains, is not really a rice at all but the seeds of a type of grass (*Zizania aquatica*). It is found growing in streams and shallow lakes of the Midwest and Mississippi valley, and in Canada.

The native North Americans greatly prized wild rice, which they called *manonim* (good berry), and even fought wars for control of the lakes in Minnesota where it grew. Until quite recently, the traditional Indian method of harvesting by canoe—manually bending over the grass heads and knocking the seed into the boat—was still in use. Now wild rice can be cultivated and picked by machines, which has led to a reduction in the previously high price.

Wild rice can be cooked in the same way as rice but using more water or other liquid. Most varieties take around 45 minutes to cook, but some new, specially-treated types take only half that time. Often served as an accompaniment to game, or mixed with rice or burghul, the strong, nutty flavour and chewy texture also make it an ideal stuffing for meat or poultry. Since it is very low in fat, it keeps better than true rice.

Beef potpie

Steak and vegetable pie

600 g braising steak
2 large onions
2 garlic cloves
3 tbsp vegetable oil
salt
freshly ground black pepper
2 tbsp flour
1 bay leaf
500 g waxy potatoes
400 g carrots
30 g parsley

For the pastry:
200 g flour
1 tsp salt
70 g butter, straight from the refrigerator
70 g lard
1 to 2 tbsp ice-cold water
1 egg yolk for glazing

Preparation time: 3 hours
(plus 45 minutes' baking time)

3,800 kJ/900 calories per portion

1 Wash and dry the steak. Remove any sinews and excess fat, and cut the meat into 2 to 3 cm cubes.

2 Peel the onions and garlic. Finely chop the onions and crush the garlic.

3 Heat the oil in a fireproof casserole or stockpot, add the meat a little at a time and brown over high heat. Add the onions and garlic, and fry until brown. Season well with salt and pepper.

4 Sprinkle the flour over the meat and fry briefly, stirring constantly. Add the bay leaf and about ¼ litre water. Cover the casserole and braise the meat over low heat for about 1 hour.

5 Meanwhile, make the pastry. Mix together the flour and salt, then rub in the butter and lard until the mixture resembles breadcrumbs. Stir in enough water to make a dough that holds together. Add another 1 to 2 tbsp ice-cold water, if necessary. Wrap in clingfilm and chill in the refrigerator for 2 to 2½ hours.

6 Peel and wash the potatoes and carrots and cut them into 3 cm dice. Add to the meat and continue to cook for a further 20 minutes.

7 Wash the parsley, shake it dry, chop finely and stir into the meat. Season generously, then transfer the mixture to a 25 to 30 cm pie dish. Leave to cool for about 30 minutes. Preheat the oven to 200°C (400°F or Mark 6).

8 On a lightly floured surface, roll out the pastry to a round or oval the same size as the top of the pie dish.

9 Cut out a design in the pastry, if liked, and reserve the trimmings to make a decorative pattern on the top. Lift the pastry and carefully lay it over the pie dish (*above*).

10 Using your fingertips, press down on the pastry evenly all the way round the edge of the dish (*above*). Whisk the egg yolk in a cup and use it to brush the pastry. If making a pattern with the pastry trimmings, stick them to the top of the pie with a little egg yolk as well. Bake the pie in the centre of the oven for about 45 minutes.

Wine: A robust red wine, such as a Cabernet Sauvignon, goes best with this hearty dish.

Note: All kinds of different ingredients are used to make pies in this way. Often, the leftovers from the Sunday roast are used to create another delicious meal the following day.

Meatloaf with bacon

Beef, pork and veal loaf cooked in bacon

Not difficult • The Midwest

Serves 4

2 slices stale white bread
2 medium-sized onions
2 garlic cloves
500 g minced beef
150 g minced pork
150 g minced veal
1 egg
1 tsp dried thyme
3 tbsp bottled medium-hot
chili sauce
salt
freshly ground black pepper
150 g streaky bacon in thin rashers

Preparation time: 30 minutes
(plus 1 hour's baking time)

3,200 kJ/760 calories per portion

1 Preheat the oven to 200°C (400°F or Mark 6). Toast the bread to dry it out a little, then crumble finely. Peel and very finely chop the onions and garlic.

2 Put the bread, onions, garlic, minced meats, egg, thyme and chili sauce in a bowl, season with salt and pepper, and mix together thoroughly. Transfer to a board and shape the mixture into a long loaf with your hands.

3 Arrange half the bacon rashers in a roasting pan or loaf tin. Lay the meat loaf on top and cover it with the rest of the bacon rashers.

4 Bake the meatloaf in the centre of the oven for about 1 hour, until cooked.

Variation: Hamloaf

Hamloaf is popular in the South. Mince 400 g cooked ham and mix with 250 g minced pork, 1 egg, 1 peeled and grated onion, 75 to 100 g fresh breadcrumbs and a little dry mustard. Season generously with salt and pepper, and shape the mixture into a loaf. Place in a roasting pan or loaf tin and bake in the centre of the oven at 200°C (400°F or Mark 6) for about 1 hour. While cooking, baste from time to time with a sauce made from 50 g brown sugar, ½ tsp dry mustard, 2 tbsp water and 2 tbsp white wine vinegar.

Note: Using minced pork and veal as well as beef gives the meatloaf a moister texture.

Yankee pot roast

Pot-roasted beef and vegetables

Serves 4

75 g rindless smoked streaky bacon
2 tbsp vegetable oil
1 kg boned and rolled brisket or
topside of beef
freshly ground black pepper
1 large onion
¼ beef stock
1 bay leaf
salt
400 g carrots
400 g small waxy potatoes
400 g small white turnips
30 g butter
2 tbsp flour
15 g fresh parsley

Preparation time: 45 minutes
(plus 2½ hours' cooking time)

2,500 kJ/600 calories per portion

1 Preheat the oven to 170°C (325°F or Mark 3). Coarsely chop the streaky bacon. Heat the vegetable oil in a fireproof casserole or stockpot and fry the bacon over medium heat until the fat runs. Remove the bacon, leaving the fat in the casserole.

2 Rub the meat all over with pepper, then brown it on all sides in the fat in the casserole over high heat.

3 Peel and finely chop the onion, add it to the meat and fry until lightly browned. Add the stock and the bay leaf and season with salt. Cover the casserole and cook on the bottom shelf of the oven for about 2 hours.

4 Wash the carrots, potatoes and turnips, peel them and cut into chunks. Add them to the meat, with a little

more water, if necessary. Cover and cook the casserole in the oven for a further 30 minutes.

5 Melt the butter in a small saucepan. Sprinkle the flour into the pan to make a roux and cook until golden-brown, stirring constantly. Remove the pan from the heat.

6 Remove the casserole from the oven and turn off the heat. Transfer the meat and vegetables to a serving dish and keep warm in the oven. Stir the roux into the meat juices, cook through briefly, then adjust the seasoning. Wash the parsley, shake it dry and chop finely, then sprinkle it over the meat and vegetables. Serve with the sauce.

Wine: A full-bodied, robust red wine goes particularly well with pot roast.

Hamburgers

Cooked patties of minced beef

Simple • All regions

Serves 4

600 g shoulder or rump steak (freshly minced by the butcher, if preferred)
salt
freshly ground black pepper
vegetable oil (if frying)

Preparation time: 30 minutes

1,400 kJ/330 calories per portion

1 Remove the sinews and excess fat from the meat. You should, however, leave a certain amount of fat. Mince the beef, but not too finely, otherwise the hamburgers will dry out.

2 Preheat the grill. Season the minced beef with salt and pepper, then shape into four round patties about 2 cm thick and smooth round the edges. Take care not to knead the meat too much, or the hamburgers will be dry.

3 Cook the hamburgers over charcoal, or under the grill, or in oil in a frying pan, for 3 to 4 minutes on each side, so that they are still slightly pink in the middle and very juicy. Cook for a little longer if you prefer them well done.

Variation: Cheeseburgers
Lay a small slice of Cheddar cheese on top of each hamburger and melt it briefly under a hot grill or in a covered frying pan.

Note: In America, these hamburgers are served in special hamburger buns, available in any supermarket. Onion rings, sliced gherkins and tomatoes, lettuce, mustard and tomato ketchup can be added to the bun with the hamburger, if wished. They can also be served with potato crisps and coleslaw (*recipe, page 40*).

Hot dogs

Frankfurters in long bread rolls

Simple • All regions

Serves 4

4 frankfurters
2 tomatoes
1 onion
2 tbsp vegetable oil
4 hot dog rolls
4 tsp made mustard
2 tbsp tomato ketchup
2 tbsp mayonnaise

Preparation time: 20 minutes

2,100 kJ/500 calories per portion

1 Heat the frankfurters in hot (not boiling) water for about 10 minutes.

2 Meanwhile, wash and thinly slice the tomatoes. Peel and thinly slice the onion, separating the slices into rings.

3 Drain the frankfurters thoroughly, then cut a shallow slit along the length of each sausage.

4 Gently heat the oil in a frying pan, add the frankfurters and fry for about 2 minutes on each side.

5 Meanwhile, preheat the grill. Cut the bread rolls open lengthwise, without cutting them right through, and toast them lightly under the grill.

6 Fill the rolls with the frankfurters, sliced tomatoes and onion rings. Add a little mustard, tomato ketchup and mayonnaise to each hot dog roll, and fold the roll back together.

Variations: Frankfurters can be grilled, rather than fried, if preferred. Sauerkraut, cheese or chili peppers can be added to the hot dog rolls.

Note: Hot dogs—like hamburgers—were served for the first time at the 1904 World Fair.

Chili con carne

Not difficult • Texas **Beef with chili peppers** *Serves 4*

1 kg topside or shoulder of beef
1 large onion
5 to 6 fresh, hot red chili peppers
(see Glossary)
5 tbsp vegetable oil
4 garlic cloves
¼ litre beef stock
1 tbsp Worcester sauce
1 tsp brown sugar
1 bay leaf
2 tsp dried thyme
½ tsp ground cumin
cayenne pepper
salt
2 to 3 tbsp fine cornmeal

Preparation time: 2 hours

2,900 kJ/670 calories per portion

1 Wash and dry the meat, and cut into 2 cm cubes, removing the sinews and any large pieces of fat.

2 Peel and finely chop the onion. Slit the chili peppers lengthwise, discard the seeds, then cut the flesh into rings.

3 Heat the oil in a heavy, wide pan. Gradually add the meat and onion, and fry over medium heat, without letting the ingredients brown too much. Peel and crush the garlic, and stir it into the meat. Stir in the chili rings.

4 Add the beef stock, Worcester sauce, sugar, bay leaf, thyme, cumin, and a little cayenne pepper and salt. Cover the pan and cook over very low heat for about 1½ hours, stirring from time to time, and adding a little water, if necessary, to prevent it drying out.

5 Before serving, stir the cornmeal into the chili to thicken it slightly. Heat through briefly and season generously. Serve the chili with corn bread (*see Step 1, page 98*).

Note: Chili con carne originates not from Mexico, as many people suppose, but from Texas. It is said to have been cooked by the women of San Antonio for members of the Texan republic militia and was prepared with minced or finely chopped meat but, as here, without kidney beans or tomatoes.

Drink: Serve chili con carne with well chilled beer. Americans find the English taste for "warm" ale rather odd!

Chili peppers and Tabasco sauce

Hot and spicy seasonings such as chili peppers and Tabasco sauce are as essential to Tex-Mex cookery as they are to the Creole and Cajun cuisines of Louisiana.

It is thought that chili peppers grew in Mexico as early as 7,000 BC. They come in all shapes, sizes and colours and, although generally the smallest tend to be the most fiery, one cannot always tell from their appearance how hot they are, so it is best to proceed with caution.

Similarly, beware of adding too much Tabasco sauce to a dish. This condiment has been produced since 1868 by a family firm on Avery Island in the Louisiana swamps. It is made to a secret recipe which includes grinding and mixing small, hot red chilies with salt, leaving them to mature for three years, then blending them with salt and vinegar before bottling. A constituent of Bloody Mary cocktails, a few drops of Tabasco sauce are enough to give a spicy flavour to numerous dishes.

Grilled T-bone steaks

T-bone steaks marinated and grilled

Simple • Texas

Serves 4

4 T-bone steaks (about 4 cm thick)
3 garlic cloves
3 to 4 tbsp vegetable oil
freshly ground black pepper
salt

**Preparation time: 30 minutes
(plus 1 hour's marinating time)**

3,400 kJ/810 calories per portion

1 Wash the steaks in cold water and pat dry. Score the fat around the edge of each steak in several places, so that they do not curl up as they cook, and place them in a shallow dish.

2 Peel and crush the garlic, then mix it with the oil and pepper to make a marinade. Brush it on the steaks, cover and leave to marinate for at least 1 hour. Prepare the barbecue.

3 Place the steaks on a rack over the charcoal. Sear for 1 minute on each side, then raise the rack and continue to cook. According to the thickness of the steaks and how you like them cooked, this will take between 10 and 28 minutes (*see Variation*).

4 Before serving, season the cooked steaks with salt and leave them to rest for a few more minutes. Serve with baked potatoes (*recipe, page 70*) and corn relish (*recipe, page 76*).

Variation: The steaks can be cooked indoors under the grill, if you prefer. Sear them in the grill pan over high heat on the top of the stove for 30 to 60 seconds on each side, then cook them under the grill for 5 minutes on each side (rare/bloody), 8 minutes each side (medium rare/pink) or 12 to 14 minutes each side (medium).

Note: T-bone and the slightly larger porterhouse steaks are cut from the sirloin. Both have T-shaped bones.

Barbecued spareribs

Spareribs cooked with spicy sauce

Not difficult • The Southwest

Serves 4

1 medium-sized onion
5 tbsp Worcester sauce
150 g tomato ketchup
a few drops of Tabasco sauce
5 tbsp brown sugar
5 tbsp wine vinegar
½ tsp dry mustard
salt
freshly ground black pepper
1.5 kg pork spareribs, cut into
individual pieces

Preparation time: 1½ hours

2,600 kJ/620 calories per portion

1 Prepare the barbecue. Peel and chop the onion. Place in a saucepan with the Worcester sauce, tomato ketchup, Tabasco sauce, brown sugar, vinegar, mustard and 5 tbsp water. Season the sauce with salt and pepper. Bring to the boil, stirring constantly, then simmer over low heat for about 5 minutes, until the onion is tender.

2 Rinse the spareribs in cold water and pat dry with paper towels. Brush thinly with some of the sauce.

3 Place the spareribs on the grill well away from the charcoal, so that they cook over low heat. According to thickness, grill for 45 to 60 minutes,

turning the ribs occasionally and brushing them from time to time with the sauce.

Variation: You can also cook spareribs in the oven. Preheat the oven to 200°C (400°F or Mark 6). Arrange the ribs side by side on a baking sheet with the meat side upwards. Roast them in the centre of the oven for 45 to 60 minutes, according to thickness. Turn them from time to time as they cook and brush with the sauce.

You may need to pour a little water on to the baking sheet to prevent the cooking juices burning.

New England boiled dinner
Traditional brisket and vegetable one-pot meal   *Serves 6*

2 kg salted brisket of beef (order in advance from the butcher)
8 small beetroot (about 1 kg)
750 g waxy potatoes
250 g baby carrots
250 g small white turnips
250 g small onions
600 g white cabbage
salt
30 g fresh parsley
horseradish sauce
prepared mustard

Preparation time: 50 minutes (plus 4 to 5 hours' cooking time)

2,500 kJ/600 calories per portion

1 Wash the brisket of beef and place it in a large saucepan. Add enough cold water to reach about 1 cm above the level of the meat.

2 Bring to the boil, skimming the scum from the surface with a slotted spoon (*above*). Simmer over very low heat, with the lid half covering the pan, for 4 to 5 hours. Add more hot water, when necessary, to prevent it boiling dry.

3 After 3 to 4 hours, when the meat is almost cooked, prepare the vegetables. (They should be ready at the same time as the meat.)

4 Wash, but do not peel, the beetroot, and place them in a saucepan of boiling water. Cover and cook over medium heat for 40 to 50 minutes, until they are just tender.

5 Peel the potatoes, baby carrots and turnips and cut them into large chunks. Peel the onions. Trim and coarsely shred the white cabbage.

6 Bring a large saucepan of salted water to the boil. Add the potatoes and onions, and cook over medium heat for about 10 minutes. Add the carrots, turnips and cabbage and cook for a further 10 minutes.

7 Pour off the water and drain the vegetables. Drain the beetroot, rinse in cold water, then peel and cut into chunks. Small beetroot should only be cut into quarters. Wash the parsley, shake dry and chop coarsely.

8 Remove the meat from the pan and carve it into slices. Arrange the sliced meat in the centre of a large serving dish, surrounded by the vegetables. Sprinkle with the chopped parsley and serve accompanied by horseradish sauce and mustard.

Note: This is one of America's oldest traditional recipes. It dates back to the days when the first settlers only possessed one large iron pot in which everything had to be cooked at the same time. It is still the custom to serve the leftovers as red flannel hash (*recipe, page 35*) for breakfast the following morning.

Make sure you allow enough time for cooking the beetroot, as cooking times can vary considerably. Cooked, unpeeled beetroot will stay hot for a long time in a covered pan.

Schnitz un knepp

Ham cooked with apple rings and dumplings

Not difficult • Pennsylvania

Serves 4

125 g dried apple rings
4 thick slices ham or gammon
(about 150 g each)
2 tbsp brown sugar

For the dumplings:
200 g plain flour
2 tsp baking powder
¼ tsp salt
1 egg
30 g butter, melted
6 to 8 tbsp milk

Preparation time: 1 hour
(plus 12 hours' soaking time)

1,900 kJ/450 calories per portion

1 Place the apple rings in a bowl and cover with ½ litre cold water. Leave to soak overnight.

2 Place the ham or gammon slices in a very wide pan with just enough water to cover. Bring the water to the boil and simmer, covered, over very low heat for about 30 minutes.

3 Add the apple rings and the soaking water to the ham. Sprinkle with the sugar, then increase the heat slightly and simmer, covered, for a further 15 minutes. The apple rings should be soft, but should not fall apart.

4 Meanwhile, to make the dumplings, mix the flour, baking powder and salt. Whisk the egg and butter together and stir into the flour. Add enough milk to make a dropping consistency.

5 Spoon the dumpling mixture on top of the apples, a tablespoonful at a time. Cover again and continue to cook for about 12 minutes. To test whether the dumplings are cooked, pierce one of them with a fine skewer. If the skewer comes out clean, they are ready.

6 Serve the ham, apples, dumplings and a little broth in soup plates.

Macaroni cheese with ham

Not difficult • All regions

Pasta and ham in a cheese sauce

Serves 4

salt
300 g short-cut macaroni
300 g cooked ham, thickly sliced
1 small onion
75 g butter
3 tbsp flour
½ litre milk
freshly ground black pepper
175 g Cheddar cheese, coarsely grated
3 tbsp fresh breadcrumbs

Preparation time: 50 minutes

3,600 kJ/860 calories per portion

1 Bring plenty of salted water to the boil in a large saucepan. Add the macaroni and cook until just *al dente*, following instructions on the packet. Dice the ham. Preheat the oven to 200°C (400°F or Mark 6).

2 Peel and finely chop the onion. Melt 45 g of the butter in a saucepan and fry the onion over medium heat until it is transparent. Add the flour and fry until golden, then gradually add the milk, stirring constantly. Season with pepper and a little salt, and simmer the sauce over low heat for about 5 minutes.

3 Thoroughly drain the pasta. Reserve 3 tbsp of the grated cheese, add the rest to the sauce and stir until it melts. Add the ham, then stir the macaroni into the sauce.

4 Transfer the macaroni cheese to a shallow baking dish. Mix together the breadcrumbs and remaining grated cheese and sprinkle it over the pasta. Flake the rest of the butter on top, then bake in the centre of the oven for about 20 minutes.

Note: Pasta has long been a favourite food in the United States. German and Italian immigrants brought many recipes with them and, following a visit to Italy, Thomas Jefferson, gourmet and third President of the United States, enthused about the many delicious pasta dishes there. Since then, many more pasta creations have become popular in America, including a Californian dish where spaghetti is served with a thickened version of the fish soup *cioppino* (*recipe, page 62*).

Beef tacos

Minced beef in taco shells with dips

1 medium-sized onion
½ sweet green pepper
2 tbsp vegetable oil
1 garlic clove
400 g minced beef
200 g tomato purée
½ tsp dried thyme
¼ tsp ground cumin
¼ tsp paprika
a few drops of Tabasco sauce
salt
freshly ground black pepper
½ small iceberg lettuce
4 small, firm tomatoes
200 g soured cream or crème fraîche
bottled medium-hot chili sauce
12 ready-made taco shells
60 g Cheddar cheese, grated

For the guacamole (avocado dip):
3 ripe avocados
juice of 2 limes
2 tomatoes
1 small onion
2 to 3 small, medium-hot chili peppers (see Glossary)
salt
15 g fresh coriander
lemon wedge and coriander leaves, to garnish (optional)

Preparation time: 1 hour

3,700 kJ/880 calories per portion

1 Peel the onion. Wash the sweet pepper and remove the stalk, ribs and seeds. Finely chop both vegetables. Heat the oil in a saucepan and stir-fry the onion and pepper over low heat until lightly browned. Peel and crush the garlic, and add to the pan.

2 Stir in the minced beef and fry until brown, then stir in the tomato purée. Add the dried thyme, cumin, paprika and Tabasco sauce. Season with salt and pepper. Simmer, uncovered, over low heat for about 20 minutes, until most of the liquid has evaporated.

3 Meanwhile, preheat the oven to 180°C (350°F or Mark 4). Trim, wash and finely shred the iceberg lettuce. Wash and halve the tomatoes, remove the seeds, then finely chop the flesh.

4 To make the guacamole, halve the avocados, remove the stones and scoop the flesh out of the shells. Purée the flesh with the lime juice in a blender or food processor. Wash the tomatoes, plunge them into boiling water, remove the skins and seeds, and chop the flesh finely. Peel and finely chop the onion.

5 Slit the chili peppers lengthwise and remove the seeds. Wash the chilies and chop finely. Stir the chopped tomatoes, onion and chili peppers into the puréed avocado and season with salt. Wash the coriander, shake it dry, chop finely and stir into the purée.

6 Transfer the guacamole to a small bowl and garnish it with the lemon wedge and coriander, if using. Put the soured cream and chilli sauce in separate bowls.

7 Heat the taco shells in the oven for 2 to 3 minutes. Meanwhile, check the meat mixture for seasoning. Fill the taco shells with the meat, lettuce, chopped tomatoes and cheese (*above*). Serve immediately with the three bowls of dips. Let everyone help themselves to the various dips.

Variation: Tortillas
Taco shells are made from cornmeal, which makes them difficult to prepare at home. If you cannot buy ready-made taco shells, you can make 12 wheat tortillas, as follows:

Mix together 250 g fine wheat flour, about 10 cl water, 1 tsp salt and 7 tbsp vegetable oil and knead to a smooth dough. Cover the dough and leave to rest for about 1 hour. Then, break off pieces the size of a table tennis ball, and roll out thinly on a lightly floured surface. Sprinkle the rolled-out tortillas with a little flour to prevent them from drying out.

Fry them in a very hot frying pan (preferably a cast-iron one) for about 30 seconds on each side, pressing flat any bubbles as they form. (Fried tortillas should have small, brown flecks.) Stack the cooked tortillas while you fry the rest. Serve with the prepared fillings.

DESSERTS AND CAKES

Americans have a weakness for sweet things. They like to nibble between meals and they also like to end a meal with something sweet. Consequently, the United States is a paradise for those with a sweet tooth, and the range of recipes for desserts and pies, or cakes and biscuits, is enormous. The variety and abundance of delicious fruit, including the more exotic ones grown in the South, also feature large in desserts, whether cut up in fruit salads or combined with pastry.

Pears, plums, peaches and apples were cultivated by the settlers—every American child knows the story of Johnny Appleseed, who wandered the country for 40 years planting apple seeds and tending the young trees.

The emphasis on baking also has its origins in the life of the 19th-century homesteaders. In such a vast land, food transportation was difficult and people made do with what they grew or what could be stored. They had plenty of flour—either maize or wheat—maple syrup or honey, fruit trees or wild nuts and berries. So, as well as bread, they baked apple, pecan or pumpkin pies, blueberry tarts, wild strawberry shortcakes and countless biscuits.

Americans also love ice cream, and the making of ice cream and sorbets goes back to the 18th century. Thomas Jefferson, the third President of the United States, owned a hand-operated ice cream machine and brought back many recipes from Italy and France.

Pecan pie

Fairly easy • The South

Classic pecan nut and maple syrup pie

Makes 12 slices

125 g butter, straight from the refrigerator, plus extra for greasing the tin
150·g plain flour
1 tbsp icing sugar
1 tbsp ice-cold water

For the filling:
4 eggs
5 tbsp maple syrup (or corn syrup, if unavailable)
45 g butter, melted
a few drops of vanilla essence
200 g shelled pecan nuts

Preparation time: 1½ hours (plus 2 hours' resting time)

1,400 kJ/330 calories per slice

1 Cut the cold butter into small dice. With cold hands, quickly knead the butter, flour, icing sugar and water to a smooth dough. Shape it into a ball, wrap in clingfilm and leave to rest in the refrigerator for 1 to 2 hours.

2 Preheat the oven to 200°C (400°F or Mark 6). Butter a 25 cm flan dish or round springform cake tin. Working fast, roll out the pastry between two layers of clingfilm to a circle about 27 to 28 cm in diameter (*See Step 3, page 124*). Discard the clingfilm and line the tin with the pastry, pressing it firmly around the edge.

3 Prick the pastry in several places with a fork. Lay a sheet of greaseproof paper over the base and fill generously with ceramic baking beans or dried lentils or beans.

4 Bake the pie shell on the bottom shelf of the oven for about 15 minutes. Remove from the oven and discard the beans and greaseproof paper. Leave the pastry to cool a little. Reduce the oven to 180°C (350°F or Mark 4).

5 To make the filling, whisk the eggs in a bowl, then stir in the maple or corn syrup, melted butter and vanilla essence. Pour the egg mixture into the pie shell. Arrange the pecan nuts on top in a circular pattern. Bake on the bottom shelf of the oven for 25 to 30 minutes. Serve the pie warm or cold.

Note: Baking a pie shell without a filling is known as "baking blind". To prevent the pastry rising as it cooks, the shell is lined with greaseproof paper and covered with ceramic baking beans or dried pulses.

Pecan nuts

The elegant and nutritious pecan nut is native to the southern states of the USA, though now also cultivated in Australia. Pecans are related to walnuts, but have a milder, sweeter, more aromatic flavour. As well as an ingredient in many sweet and savoury dishes, including ice creams and pecan pie (*see left*), they are a favourite American snack food.

Pecans grow on hickory trees which can reach a height of up to 50 metres. They are grown on large plantations in the South and Southwest, especially in Arizona and Louisiana. They have a high fat content and were a vital source of nourshment to the native Americans who once lived on the banks of the Mississippi River.

Enclosed in a smooth brown shell, the oily kernel of the pecan nut develops in two separate halves. The nuts are available in their shells in the autumn, and shelled all year round. When buying unshelled pecans, choose those that have unblemished, uncracked shells and that do not rattle when shaken.

Key lime pie

Lime cream pie with a meringue topping

A little more complex • Florida

Makes 10 to 12 slices

125 g butter, straight from the refrigerator, plus extra for greasing the dish
150 g plain flour
1 tbsp icing sugar
1 tbsp ice-cold water

For the cream filling:
6 egg yolks
400 g can sweetened condensed milk
4 to 5 limes

For the meringue:
6 egg whites
175 g sugar
¼ tsp cream of tartar

Preparation time: 1¾ hours
(plus 2 hours' resting time)

1,100 kJ/260 calories per slice (if serving 12)

1 Cut the butter into dice. With cold hands, quickly knead the butter, flour, icing sugar and water to a dough and shape into a ball. Wrap in clingfilm and refrigerate for 1 to 2 hours.

2 Preheat the oven to 200°C (400°F or Mark 6). Generously butter a 25 cm flan dish or springform cake tin.

3 Working fast, roll out the pastry between two layers of clingfilm to a circle about 27 to 28 cm in diameter (*above*). Discard the clingfilm and line the tin with the pastry, pressing it firmly around the edge.

4 Prick the pastry in several places with a fork. Lay a sheet of greaseproof paper over the base and fill generously with dried lentils or beans.

5 Bake the pie shell on the bottom shelf of the oven for about 15 minutes. Remove from the oven, discard the beans or lentils, and greaseproof paper, and bake the shell for a further 10 minutes. Allow the pastry to cool a little. Reduce the oven temperature to 180°C (350°F or Mark 4).

6 To make the cream filling, place the egg yolks in a bowl. Add the condensed milk and beat until thick.

7 Rinse the limes in hot water and pat dry. Finely grate the rind of two of the limes and add it to the cream. Squeeze the limes, measure about 12.5 cl of the juice and pour it into the cream. Stir briefly, then pour the mixture into the pie shell, smoothing the surface. Bake the pie on the bottom shelf of the oven for about 20 minutes.

8 Meanwhile, whisk the egg whites until stiff, then add the sugar a little at a time, and trickle in the cream of tartar. Reduce the oven temperature to 150°C (300°F or Mark 2). Pile the meringue on top of the pie using a tablespoon and bake in the oven for about 15 to 20 minutes, or until the meringue is golden-brown.

9 Leave the pie to cool thoroughly and serve, preferably the same day.

Note: Florida cooks prefer to make their famous speciality with the excellently flavoured tiny limes grown on the Florida Keys, but any limes can be used.

Bread pudding with whiskey

Fairly easy • Louisiana

Bread and sultana pudding with whiskey sauce

Serves 6 to 8

butter for the baking dish
200 g stale white baguettes
40 cl milk
2 eggs
150 g sugar
75 g sultanas or raisins
a few drops of vanilla essence

For the sauce:
70 g butter
70 g sugar
1 egg
7 tbsp Bourbon whiskey

Preparation time: 20 minutes
(plus 1 hour's cooking time)

1,600 kJ/380 calories per portion
(if serving 8)

1 Preheat the oven to 200°C (400°F or Mark 6). Butter a 1 litre oval baking dish. Break the baguettes into small pieces, place them in a bowl, pour the milk over the bread and leave to soak for about 15 minutes.

2 In another bowl, whisk the eggs and sugar until thick and creamy. Stir in the sultanas and vanilla essence.

3 Add the egg and sultana mixture to the soaked bread and stir thoroughly. Transfer to the greased baking dish and smooth the surface.

4 Place the baking dish in a roasting pan, with enough boiling water to reach half way up the side of the dish. Bake on the lowest shelf of the oven for about 1 hour.

5 Meanwhile, to make the sauce, dice the butter into a bowl and set it over a saucepan of gently simmering water until melted. Add the sugar and egg, and continue to stir until the sauce thickens. Stir in the whiskey a little at a time. Remove the bowl from the pan of hot water and allow the sauce to cool until just warm.

6 Serve the bread pudding straight from the oven, accompanied by the warm whiskey sauce.

Applesauce cake

Iced cake made with puréed apples and spices

A little more complex • The Northeast

Makes 9 slices

butter for greasing the baking tin
100 g raisins
100 g shelled walnuts
500 g cooking apples
125 g butter, softened
130 g brown sugar
1 egg
a few drops of vanilla essence
250 g plain flour
1 tbsp baking powder
¼ tsp freshly grated nutmeg
¼ tsp ground cloves
½ tsp ground cinnamon

For the icing:
300 g brown sugar
75 g butter • 10 cl double cream
a few drops of vanilla essence

Preparation time: 50 minutes
(plus 45 minutes' cooking time)

2,700 kJ/640 calories per slice

1 Preheat the oven to 180°C (350°F or Mark 4). Grease a 20 by 30 cm baking tin with plenty of butter. Cover the raisins with boiling water and leave to soak briefly. Chop the walnuts.

2 Peel and chop the apples, then simmer them with a little water until tender—about 10 minutes. Purée the apples in a blender or food processor.

3 Beat the butter and sugar in a bowl until creamy. Stir in the egg, followed by the apple purée, walnuts and vanilla essence. Sift the flour with the baking powder and spices, and stir into the mixture. Stir in the drained raisins.

4 Transfer the mixture to the baking tin and smooth the surface. Bake in the centre of the oven for about 45 minutes. Turn out and cool on a wire rack.

5 To make the icing, place the sugar, butter and double cream in a saucepan and cook over medium heat for 3 to 5 minutes, until melted. Continue to stir until the mixture caramelizes. Test by dropping a little of the syrup into cold water. If it is ready, it will immediately form a soft ball. Take care, because caramel burns very easily.

6 Transfer the caramel to a mixing bowl, add the vanilla essence and stir vigorously. Spread the warm icing over the cake with a spoon. If the icing is already beginning to set, dip the spoon in hot water first. Leave the icing to set, then serve the cake cut into slices.

Note: If this recipe is too sweet for your taste, omit the caramel icing and simply sprinkle the top of the cake with icing sugar.

Strawberry shortcake

Fairly easy • New England

Shortcake layered with strawberries and cream

Makes 12 slices

butter for greasing the tin
350 g plain flour
1 tbsp baking powder
salt
freshly grated nutmeg
125 g sugar
175 g butter, straight from the refrigerator
12.5 cl double cream
30 g butter, melted

For the filling and topping:
1 kg strawberries
50 to 100 g sugar (according to taste)
2 tbsp lemon juice
20 cl double cream
icing sugar for dusting

Preparation time: 1¼ hours

1,600 kJ/380 calories per slice

1 Preheat the oven to 200°C (400°F or Mark 6). Carefully butter a 22 cm round springform cake tin. Sift the flour, baking powder, salt and nutmeg into a bowl, and mix with the sugar.

2 Dice the 175 g butter, add to the flour mixture and blend with your fingertips to a crumb-like consistency.

3 Add the cream and continue stirring to make a smooth dough. Briefly knead the dough, then divide it into two portions. On a floured work surface, roll out each portion to a circle about 22 cm in diameter. Place them one on top of the other in the cake tin.

4 Bake in the centre of the oven for about 30 minutes, until golden-brown. Test to see if it is cooked by inserting a fine skewer into the centre; if the skewer comes out clean, it is ready.

5 Loosen the shortcake from the edge of the tin, then remove the spring-clip rim and let the cake cool a little. Split the cake in half crosswise while still warm, then sprinkle the cut surfaces with the melted butter.

6 Wash and hull the strawberries, and reserve a few for decoration. Chop the rest and mix with the sugar and lemon juice. Cover the bottom shortcake with two thirds of the strawberries, place the other shortcake on top and press gently. Spread the rest of the chopped strawberries on top. Whip the cream until stiff and spread it over the cake. Halve the reserved strawberries and use to decorate the cake. Dust with a little icing sugar.

Variation: Whipped cream can be spread over the bottom shortbread layer before adding the strawberries.

Angel food cake

Not difficult • All regions

Light-as-air sponge cake made with egg whites

Makes 12 slices

160 g egg whites (from 5 or 6 eggs)
¼ tsp cream of tartar
¼ tsp salt
150 g caster sugar
½ tsp vanilla essence
90 g plain flour
icing sugar for dusting

Preparation time: 1 hour

480 kJ/110 calories per slice

1 Preheat the oven to 180°C (350°F or Mark 4). Whisk the egg whites in a large bowl until frothy, add the cream of tartar and salt, and continue to whisk until the egg whites are stiff.

2 Trickle about 50 g sugar into the egg whites a little at a time. Fold in the vanilla essence and 1 tsp cold water.

3 Mix the remaining 100 g sugar with the flour, and gradually sprinkle the mixture over the egg whites, folding it in very gently with a metal spoon.

4 Transfer immediately to a special angel cake tin or a non-stick, tubular tin, and bake in the centre of the oven for about 30 minutes.

5 Place the tin upside down on a wire rack and leave the cake to cool in the tin. When the cake is completely cold, carefully remove it from the tin. Serve sprinkled with icing sugar.

Note: Whisk the egg yolks and freeze them in a plastic container, ready to use for another dish.

Old-fashioned ice cream

Not difficult • Philadelphia

Traditional vanilla ice cream

Serves 6

1 vanilla pod
30 cl single cream
80 g sugar
salt
20 cl double cream

Preparation time: 30 minutes (plus 1 hour's cooling time and 4 hours' freezing time)

1,500 kJ/360 calories per portion

1 Slit the vanilla pod open lengthwise and scrape out the black pulp with a small sharp knife. Place the pod and pulp in a pan with the single cream, sugar and a little salt and heat through over low heat, stirring constantly, until the sugar dissolves. Do not boil.

2 Take the saucepan off the heat and leave the mixture to cool, then stir in the double cream, mixing well. Discard the vanilla pod.

3 Transfer the cooled mixture to a freezer-proof bowl. Cover, and freeze for at least 4 hours, turning the sides to the middle when they begin to harden. When the ice cream is solid, beat well, then return to the freezer.

Variation: Chocolate ice cream
Heat about 50 cl double cream in a saucepan over low heat. Add about 125 g chopped plain chocolate, stir until the chocolate has melted, then flavour the mixture with 1 tbsp ground vanilla or a few drops of vanilla essence, cover and freeze.

Note: Although ice cream is extremely popular throughout all of the United States, Philadelphia is known as the "ice cream capital" of the world.

Because it is America's favourite dessert, there are many different flavours for ice cream connoisseurs to enjoy. Quite a few households own an ice cream maker, so that preparation of this refreshing treat is simple.

Bananas Foster

Quick • Louisiana

Bananas flambéed in rum and liqueur

Serves 4

4 portions vanilla ice cream (about 200 g)
50 g butter
3 tbsp soft brown sugar
¼ tsp ground cinnamon
4 small bananas
4 tbsp banana-flavoured liqueur
4 tbsp rum or whiskey

Preparation time: 10 minutes

1,100 kJ/260 calories per portion

1 Divide the ice cream between four plates. Heat the butter with the sugar and cinnamon in a wide frying pan, stirring until the butter and sugar have melted.

2 Peel the bananas, halve them lengthwise and, if you like, crosswise. Heat them through in the frying pan for 3 minutes, sprinkling with the syrup.

3 Add the banana-flavoured liqueur and the rum or whiskey, and set alight immediately with a long match. When the flames have died down, serve the bananas with the ice cream.

Note: This dessert was named after Richard Foster, a customer at New Orleans' Brenan's Restaurant where the dish was created. In Hawaii it is known as "Pele's bananas" after Pele, the goddess of the islands.

Provided you have all ingredients to hand, you can flambé the bananas and assemble the dessert immediately before serving, without having to spend too long in the kitchen. Just before the main course, take the ice cream out of the freezer and put it in the refrigerator so that it softens slightly and is easy to divide into individual portions.

Pumpkin pie

Classic, spicy pumpkin pie

For the pastry:
250 g plain flour
½ tsp salt • ½ tsp sugar
100 g coconut oil or lard
1 egg
2 tbsp fruit or cider vinegar
3 to 4 tbsp ice-cold water
butter for greasing the dish

For the filling:
1 pumpkin (about 700 g) or 400 g
trimmed pumpkin flesh
12.5 cl double cream
12.5 cl milk
175 g soft brown sugar
3 eggs
¼ tsp ground cinnamon
ground cloves • ground ginger
freshly grated nutmeg

Preparation time: 1¼ hours
(plus 1 hour's baking time)

1,400 kJ/330 calories per portion

1 To make the pastry, knead the flour, salt, sugar, coconut oil or lard, egg, vinegar and iced water to a dough, working fast. Shape into a ball, wrap it in clingfilm and leave to rest in the refrigerator for at least 1 hour.

2 Meanwhile, to make the filling, peel the pumpkin and cut it into cubes. Place them in a saucepan with about 10 cl water, cover, and cook over low heat for about 15 minutes, until tender.

3 Drain the cooked pumpkin very thoroughly in a colander, then mix it with the cream, milk, brown sugar, eggs, cinnamon, a little ground cloves and ginger, and grated nutmeg.

4 Preheat the oven to 200°C (400°F or Mark 6). Generously grease a 25 cm round pie dish. Roll out the pastry between two layers of clingfilm to a circle 26 cm in diameter (*see Step 3, page 124*). Discard the clingfilm and line the pie dish with the pastry. Cut off any pastry hanging over the side of the dish and press the edges down.

5 Prick the pie shell several times with a fork. Pour the filling into the shell, and bake in the centre of the oven for about 1 hour.

Peach cobbler

Almond-flavoured peach pie

Fairly easy • The South

Serves 8

For the filling:
8 large peaches
125 g brown sugar
3 to 4 drops of almond essence
30 g butter, melted
1 tbsp flour

For the pastry:
150 g plain flour
salt
6 tbsp sugar
freshly grated nutmeg
60 g butter
7 to 8 tbsp milk

20 cl cream

Preparation time: 45 minutes
(plus 45 minutes' baking time)

1,300 kJ/310 calories per portion

1 Preheat the oven to 200°C (400°F or Mark 6). Wash the peaches. Bring the water to the boil in a saucepan and simmer the peaches over low heat for 3 to 4 minutes. Remove the peaches from the water, peel and halve, and remove the stones.

2 Cut the peach halves into thick wedges and mix with the brown sugar, almond essence, melted butter and the 1 tbsp flour. Transfer to a 15 by 20 cm ovenproof dish.

3 To make the pastry, mix the flour, salt, sugar and a little freshly grated nutmeg. Dice the butter and, with your fingertips, knead it into the flour. Add enough milk to make a smooth, but not sticky, dough.

4 On a lightly floured work surface, roll out the pastry to make a lid for the dish. Lay the pastry over the peaches, pressing it down around the edge of the dish. Bake in the centre of the oven for about 45 minutes, until golden-brown. Whip the cream until stiff. Serve the cobbler warm or cold with the whipped cream.

Variation: Morello cobbler
Instead of peaches, you can use morello cherries. Before baking, you will need to thicken the cherries with cornflour or arrowroot.

Cheesecake

Rich, cooked, lemon-flavoured cheesecake

Fairly easy • All regions

Serves 12

175 g digestive biscuits
2 tbsp sugar
½ tsp ground cinnamon
75 g butter, plus melted butter for greasing the cake tin

For the filling:
700 g cream cheese • 175 g sugar
6 eggs • 400 g soured cream
1 tsp vanilla essence
3 tbsp cornflour • 1 tbsp lemon juice
1 tbsp grated lemon rind

Preparation time: 45 minutes
(plus 1 hour's baking time and
12 hours' resting time)

2,100 kJ/500 calories per portion

1 Finely crumble the biscuits in a food processor or place them in a plastic bag and crush them with a rolling pin. Mix with the sugar and cinnamon.

2 Melt the butter in a saucepan, then stir it into the crumbs. Brush the base of a 28 cm round, springform cake tin with melted butter. Press the crumbs evenly over the bottom of the tin. Leave to chill in the refrigerator. Preheat the oven to 200°C (400°F or Mark 6).

3 To make the filling, mix the cream cheese and sugar. Separate the eggs and stir the yolks into the cheese mixture, one at a time, followed by the soured cream. Mix thoroughly.

4 Stir the vanilla essence, cornflour, lemon juice and grated lemon rind into the cream cheese. Whisk the egg whites until stiff and fold them gently into the cheese mixture.

5 Spread the filling evenly over the crumb crust. Bake the cheesecake in the centre of the oven for about 1 hour. As soon as it begins to colour, cover with greaseproof paper.

6 Turn off the heat and leave the cake to stand for a further 15 minutes in the oven with the door half open. Leave the cheesecake to rest overnight, if possible, before removing from the tin and cutting into slices.

Brownies

Chocolate and walnut brownies

Quick • All regions

Makes 20 brownies

100 g plain chocolate
125 g butter, softened
150 g soft brown sugar
2 eggs
1 tsp vanilla essence
100 g plain flour
½ tsp baking powder
salt
150 g shelled walnuts
butter for greasing the tin

Preparation time: 20 minutes
(plus 30 minutes' baking time)

780 kJ/190 calories per brownie

1 Preheat the oven to 200°C (400°F or Mark 6). Coarsely chop the chocolate, then melt it in a heatproof bowl set over a pan of gently simmering water, stirring constantly. When the chocolate has melted, remove the bowl from the pan of water and set it aside briefly.

2 In a bowl, mix the softened butter and brown sugar until creamy, using a hand whisk. Stir in the eggs, vanilla essence and melted chocolate.

3 Sift the flour, baking powder and a little salt together in a bowl. Chop the shelled walnuts. Mix together the walnuts, chocolate mixture and flour mixture, and stir well.

4 Grease a 20 cm square baking tin. Pour the batter into the prepared tin and bake in the centre of the oven for about 30 minutes, until a fine skewer inserted into the centre comes out almost clean (*see Note*).

5 Turn out on to a wire cooling rack and leave until completely cold. To serve, cut into 5 cm squares.

Note: It is important not to overcook brownies. They should be moist and slightly chewy on the inside—they will firm up as they cool.

Chocolate chip cookies

Simple • Massachusetts **Biscuits with nuts and chocolate chips** *Makes 25 cookies*

125 g softened butter
70 g white sugar
70 g brown sugar
¼ tsp salt
a few drops of vanilla essence
2 eggs
150 g plain flour
1 tsp baking powder
75 g shelled pecan nuts or walnuts
100 g chocolate chips or chopped plain chocolate

Preparation time: 45 minutes

550 kJ/130 calories per cookie

1 Preheat the oven to 200°C (400°F or Mark 6). Line two baking sheets with greaseproof paper.

2 Beat the butter, white and brown sugars, salt and vanilla essence in a bowl until creamy. Stir in the eggs. Sift the flour with the baking powder and stir it into the creamed mixture.

3 Chop the pecan nuts or walnuts and stir them into the batter with the chocolate chips or chopped chocolate.

4 Spoon the batter, a tablespoonful at a time, onto the lined baking sheets, leaving plenty of space between them. Bake them in two batches in the centre of the oven for 10 to 12 minutes. Leave to cool on a wire rack.

Note: These cookies are also known as "Toll house cookies" after the Toll House Restaurant, situated half way between Boston and New Bedford, where the original chocolate chip cookie was created. They are enjoyed throughout America as a dessert or snack. Because they are so popular, there are speciality shops that sell only freshly baked cookies.

Chocolate fudge

Takes a little time · New England

Creamy chocolate fudge with nuts

Makes 20 squares

250 g icing sugar
30 g cocoa powder
100 g butter
5 tbsp milk
40 g pecan nuts or walnuts
a few drops of vanilla essence
butter for greasing the tin

Preparation time: 45 minutes
(plus 2 hours' setting time)

190 kJ/45 calories per square

1 Sift the icing sugar and cocoa powder into a saucepan. Add the butter and milk and bring to the boil, stirring constantly. Reduce the heat and simmer over very low heat for about 20 minutes, continuing to stir.

2 Finely chop the pecan nuts or walnuts, then stir them into the fudge, together with the vanilla essence.

3 Generously butter a 20 cm square baking tin. Pour the fudge into the tin and smooth the surface. Leave to cool and set for about 2 hours.

4 Turn the fudge out of the tin on to a chopping board and cut into 2.5 cm squares. Store in an airtight tin with a close fitting lid, to prevent the fudge drying out.

Variation: There are many fudge variations in the USA but chocolate is the most popular flavour. Cocoa powder or plain chocolate may be used. Fudge is often sweetened with golden syrup or maple syrup, instead of sugar.

Suggested Menus

The order of the menu is the same in America as it is in Great Britain. The starter is followed by the main course accompanied by side dishes, with a dessert to finish.

Evening dinner is the main meal of the day. Lunch tends to be no more than a snack, perhaps a hamburger or hot dogs, salad or pizza, but more often different types of sandwiches with all kinds of imaginative fillings.

Most people drink soft drinks, such as orange juice or cola, or beer with their meals. In the South, iced tea is a favourite refresher. Wine is becoming increasingly popular and many states now produce excellent examples. Californian wines especially have acquired a fine reputation in Europe, and are available in many supermarkets and off-licences.

The following menus, which have been put together from recipes in this book, are suggestions for various occasions.

Simple dishes, and items such as fruit, for which there are no recipes, are marked with an asterisk.

Quick menus

Caesar salad	42
Creamed scallops	86
Fresh fruit*	—
Steamed clams	49
Southern fried chicken	100
French fries*	—
Ice cream*	—
Iceberg salad*	—
Catfish with hush puppies	89
Bananas Foster	130

Spring menus

Cioppino	62
Beef tacos	118
Fruit salad*	—
Steamed clams	49
Steamed salmon steaks	93
Steamed vegetables*	—
Ice cream with fruit*	—

Summer menus

Chilled avocado soup	52
Fish with orange	93
Key lime pie	124
Lomi lomi	47
Stuffed quail	102
Pineapple salad*	—

Autumn menus

Pumpkin soup	58
Yankee pot roast	107
Applesauce cake	127
Peanut soup	54
Schnitz un knepp	116
Pumpkin pie	132

Winter menus

Waldorf salad	40
Beef potpie	104
Bananas Foster	130
Peanut soup	54
Chili con carne	110
Tortillas (variation)	118
Applesauce cake	127

Fish and seafood menus

Shrimp cocktail	47
Caesar salad	42
Crab cakes	84
Angel food cake	129
Fresh fruit salad*	—
Chilled melon	—
Seafood gumbo	63
Jambalaya	85
Bread pudding with whiskey	126

Regional menus

Louisiana

Oysters Rockefeller	48
Jambalaya	85
Bread pudding with whiskey	126

The South (Soul food)

Catfish with hush puppies	89
Steamed vegetables*	—
Water melon*	—

The Midwest

Coleslaw	40
Grilled T-bone steaks	112
French fries*	—
Fried onion rings (variation)	78
Peaches or melon*	—

The Southwest

Black bean soup	57
Chili con carne	110
Fresh fruit*	—

New England

Corn chowder	57
Yankee pot roast	107
Strawberry shortcake	129

Festive menus

Americans always serve turkey at Thanksgiving in November, when the whole family or a group of friends meet for a celebration. Unlike Europe, there is no typical Christmas dish. However, Americans traditionally celebrate New Year with a Hoppin' John dinner. A coin is hidden in the main dish and whoever finds it will have good luck in the coming year.

Hoppin' John dinner

Oysters Rockefeller	48
Hoppin' John	68
Candied sweet potatoes	72
Green vegetables*	—

Thanksgiving dinner

Pumpkin soup	58
Roast turkey	98
Candied sweet potatoes	72
Steamed vegetables*	—
Cranberry sauce	77
Applesauce cake	127

Dinner party menus

Baked bean dinner

Clam chowder	53
Boston baked beans	60
Baked ham (see *Succotash*; Note)	78
Corn relish	76
Angel food cake	129

New England boiled dinner

Steamed clams	49
New England boiled dinner	114
Corn relish	76
Pumpkin pie	132

Lobster dinner

Chilled avocado soup	52
Caesar salad	42
Lobster Newburg	82
Peach cobbler	133
Old-fashioned ice cream	130

Menus to prepare in advance

Waldorf salad	40
Chicken à la king	100
Rice*	—
Pecan pie	122

Chilled avocado soup	52
Crab cakes	84
Strawberry shortcake	129

Brunch

Brunch, eaten in the late morning, consists of dishes from breakfast and lunch, the meals it replaces. Usually, there is a selection of dishes from which guests can choose.

Eggs with hash browns	34
Doughnuts	31
Toast, butter and marmalade*	—
Corn chowder	57
Oysters Rockefeller	48
Shrimp cocktail	47
Macaroni cheese with ham	117
Strawberry shortcake	129
Fresh fruit*	—

Picnic

Blueberry muffins	31
Bagels	32
Waldorf salad	40
Coleslaw	40
Chicken salad	43
Salt cod balls	90
Southern fried chicken	100
Meatloaf with bacon	106
Pumpkin pie	132
Cheesecake	134
Chocolate fudge	137
Fresh fruit*	—

Barbecue

Barbecued spareribs	112
Grilled T-bone steaks	112
Corn relish	76
Stuffed baked potatoes	70
Blackened fish	88
Vegetables*	—
Corn on the cob	75
Pecan pie	122
Fresh fruit*	—

Glossary

This glossary is intended as a brief guide to some less familiar cookery terms and ingredients, as well as words and items found on American menus.

Abalone: an edible gastropod mollusc found in the Pacific Ocean.

Andouille: spicy, smoked pork sausage, a favourite of the Cajuns. The fieriness of the sausage is tempered by brushing it with maple syrup during the smoking process. Also known as *chaurice*, it is similar to the Spanish *chorizo*.

Bagel: ring-shaped yeast roll with shiny crust and a dense, slightly chewy, texture. Bagels are poached before being baked. In America, bagels filled with lox (a type of smoked salmon) and cream cheese are a traditional Jewish snack.

Black-eyed beans (also called black-eyedpeas): Small, cream-coloureddried beans with a black "eye" in the middle. America's most common bean variety. Another name for them is cowpeas.

Blueberries: deep blue, edible berries of the family *Vaccinium* that grow wild all over North America. Related to European bilberries, but larger and sweeter, they are made into preserves and pies as well as used to flavour ice cream.

Brick: strongly flavoured cheese, one of the few of purely American origin. Many of the best cheeses produced in America are adaptations of classic European ones, such as Cheddar and Camembert.

Brunch: a combination of breakfast and lunch, served half way between the two.

Cajun: a Louisiana descendant of the immigrant Acadians—French settlers expelled from eastern Canada by the British in the 18th century; also the name of their highly seasoned style of cooking and the French dialect they speak.

Catfish: freshwater fish with a broad head, smooth skin and long barbels that look like cat's whiskers. Catfish are now extensively farmed in America—often in flooded paddy fields—and are a favourite in Southern cooking. *See also* Wolf-fish.

Chinook salmon (also called king salmon): the biggest and finest of the ocean-going salmon, found on the Pacific Northwest. *See also* Salmon.

Chesapeake crabs: crabs caught in the bay of the same name, on the Atlantic coast between Virginia and Maryland.

Chili peppers: a variety of hot red or green peppers of the capsicum family. Chilies contain volatile oils that can irritate the skin and cause eyes to burn, so handle them with caution and always wash your hands immediately after using them. The seeds of the chili are its hottest part and this should be taken into account when using either fresh or dried chili peppers. *See also page 111.*

Chowder: a thick soup or stew, often made with seafood.

Clambake: a traditional beach barbecue, especially popular in New England. The native Americans first showed the early settlers how to build a grill on the beach to roast corn, fish and shellfish. To make the grill, a deep hole is dug in the sand and filled with stones and wood. The wood is set alight, more stones are added and left until red hot. Seaweed is piled on to the hot stones and the food, wrapped in seaweed, is placed on top, moistened with seawater and cooked in the steam.

Clams: various bivalve molluscs with grey to white shells. Many different varieties and sizes are found both in the Pacific and Atlantic. Often called by the American Indian name quahog, the hard-shell clams native to the US east coast are known as littlenecks, cherrystones and chowder clams, depending on size. They are also found in Britain, France and Ireland, along with venus, carpet shell and razor clams. Also popular with Americans are soft-shell clams such as the Atlantic longneck and steamer clams or the Pacific manila clams.

Conch: large edible sea snails, popular in Florida and the Caribbean, eaten raw in salads, stir-fried or used in chowders.

Corn: cereal native to America, known as maize or corn on the cob in Europe. A staple food since the time of the Pilgrim Fathers, corn, or maize, is eaten as a vegetable, used as animal feed and ground into flour.

Cornflour: a starchy white powder made from maize kernels, used to thicken many puddings and sauces.

Cornmeal: White or yellow flour made from ground dried maize kernels. Until wheat flour became widely available in America, cornmeal was the principal flour used for baking.

Crab: crustacean with five pairs of jointed legs, the first of which have pincers. There are many different kinds of crab in the USA. Because of their high perishability, crabs are sold live or cooked. *See also individual crab names.*

Cranberries: red berries of the family *Vaccinium*, used to make preserves and the traditional sauce accompaniment to the Thanksgiving turkey. Related to blueberries, American cranberries are larger than the European ones.

Crawfish: American name for freshwater crayfish, resembling tiny lobsters. Caught in large numbers in the bayous of Louisiana, they are much used in Creole and Cajun cuisine.

Creole: in Louisiana, the term refers to a person of French ancestry or the French dialect spoken by such a person. Creole cuisine is the Louisiana style of cooking, particularly notable in New Orleans.

Dungeness crab: plate-sized crab with tender meat, native to the cold waters of the Pacific northwest and Alaska.

Dutch brown beans: a variety of kidney bean used in dishes such as Boston baked beans. Haricot beans are a good substitute.

French fries: deep-fried, thinly cut potato chips that are a popular side dish throughout America.

Grapefruit: yellow or pink-fleshed citrus fruit, grown in southern USA, including large plantations in Florida and Texas.

Gravlax: dry-cured marinated salmon.

Grits: *see* Hominy grits.

Gumbo: a soup or stew made from a wide variety of ingredients, especially seafood, and often thickened with okra (the name "gumbo" comes from the Congolese word for okra). Popular throughout the Southern states, Creole gumbos sometimes omit the okra.

Happy hour: a period, usually between 5 and 7 pm, when cut-price cocktails are served in hotels and bars, often with free cocktail snacks.

Hominy: treated, hulled maize kernels, cooked and served as a side dish, or ground into grits, (*see below*). Can also be bought in cans.

Hominy grits (also called grits): coarsely ground dry hominy (*see above*). Often cooked with water or milk to make a kind of porridge and served for breakfast in the Southern states.

King crab: one of the largest members of the crab family. Specimens weighing up to 10 kg mostly come from Alaska.

Liederkranz: a strongly flavoured cheese, one of the few cheeses of purely American origin. *See also* Brick.

Lime: green, vitamin-rich citrus fruit. Cultivated on plantations in Florida, those that grow on the Florida keys have a particularly high aromatic flavour.

Lobster: crustacean, prized for its fine-flavoured flesh, found in many oceans and, in the United States, mainly on the Atlantic east coast; the best come from Maine. *See also* Spiny lobster.

Lox: brine-cured smoked salmon, slightly saltier than ordinary smoked salmon. *See also* Bagels.

Maple syrup: a syrup made from the sap of the sugar maple tree. *See also page 29.*

Mint julep: famous Southern cocktail, consisting of fresh mint, ice cubes, sugar syrup and whiskey.

Muffin: in America, a small, sweet bread bun, baked in a special cup-shaped tin.

Okra (also called ladies' fingers): the green, finger-like pods of a plant indigenous to the African continent and brought to America by the slaves. Okra is eaten as a vegetable and in the Southern states it is used as a thickening agent in stews such as gumbo.

Oyster: a bivalve mollusc with two dissimilar shells found all over the world and now extensively farmed. On the US Atlantic and Pacific coasts, as in Europe, oysters are popularly eaten raw. Along the Southern seaboard they are often served cooked, since those caught locally have less flavour.

Peanuts (also called groundnuts): not nuts but the fruit of a leguminous plant related to peas and beans, which grow underground. Widely cultivated in the southern regions of the United States, half the national crop is used to make peanut butter. *See also page 54.*

Pecan: a nut native to the United States, similar in appearance to a walnut, used in sweet and savoury dishes. *See also page 123.*

Pumpkin: an orange-fleshed winter squash grown all over the United States. *See also page 59.*

Rainbow trout: freshwater trout found in the rivers and streams of America and the trout species most commonly farmed, also in Europe.

Salmon: a sea fish, weighing from 3 to 13 kg, which returns to the freshwater river or lake where it was born in order to spawn. One of America's favourite fish, it is now also extensively farmed. The best wild salmon are found in the Pacific Northwest, including Chinook, or king salmon, sockeye and chum. The centre of the salmon industry is in Seattle.

Scallion: spring onion.

Scallop: a bivalve mollusc found in oceans worldwide; the smaller scallop is called bay scallop in America, queen scallop in the UK. The white nut of meat (actually the adductor muscle) and the orange roe, or coral, are edible, though

Americans more often eat scallops without the coral. *See also page 86.*

Shrimp: in America, prawns as well as shrimps are referred to as "shrimp". A wide variety of shrimp of all sizes can be found along both the Pacific and Atlantic coasts.

Soft-shell crab: the name given to a blue crab after it has shed its hard shell (between April and May) and has not yet grown a new one. Fished off the coasts of Maryland, Virginia and the Carolinas, soft-shelled crabs are eaten whole and considered a special delicacy. They are now available here frozen or canned.

Sourdough: a raising agent for bread made with potatoes or yeast that is left to ferment and still widely used in Alaska, Hawaii and the western states as a raising agent for bread, pancakes and waffles. In the past, pioneers and cowboys always travelled with a small amount of sourdough, which was used as a starter for bread whenever needed.

Spiny lobster (also called crawfish, rock lobster or langouste): a crustacean similar to a lobster but without the huge claws of the true lobster. Spiny lobsters weighing up to 1 kg are caught off the west coast of Florida.

Squash: a member of the *cucurbitaceae* family. The word squash comes from the American Indian word *askutasquash* meaning "eaten raw". Winter squashes have hard, inedible skins and include pumpkin, butternut, hubbard and chayotte. The less mature summer squashes have softer skins and can be eaten unpeeled; they include vegetable marrows, courgettes, patty pans and crooknecks.

Stone crab: a short-tailed crab, popular in Florida.

Sweetcorn: another name for corn, or maize, usually referring to the whole ripe young cobs eaten as a vegetable, or the kernels sold in cans. *See also* Corn.

Sweet potato: either one of two types of nutritious tuber, one with yellowish mealy flesh, the other with a moist, sweet, orange flesh. The latter is often sold as yam, but should not be confused with the true yam. *See also page 73 and* Yam.

Tabasco sauce: Hot, piquant condiment containing chili peppers, much used in Southern, especially Creole, cooking. *See also page 111.*

Taro (also called eddo): large, edible underground tuber, native to Southeast Asia and closely related to the Indonesian dasheen. Rich in starch, it is cultivated in the Pacific islands and is an important staple in Hawaii, where it is often made into a puréed dish called *poi* and served at a *luau*, or festive meal; the leaves are also edible.

Tex-Mex: the cooking style of the Southwest region of the United States, combining Texan and Mexican food.

Thanksgiving: the fourth Thursday in November, declared an official US holiday in 1961. The first Thanksgiving was celebrated by the Pilgrim Fathers who gave a festive meal, including roast turkey, to thank the native Americans for helping them to survive their first year.

Vanilla essence or extract: a flavouring obtained from vanilla pods and used in cakes and desserts. Vanilla extract used

in the United States is sometimes milder than that used in Europe. Alternatively use vanilla sugar, *see below.*

Vanilla sugar: sugar flavoured by placing a whole vanilla pod in a closed container of sugar for about a week. It can also be bought in packets from supermarkets.

Whiskey: a term that in the United States usually refers to Bourbon whiskey. Produced mainly in the Southern states, it is distilled from a mixture of maize, malt and rye.

Wild rice: The long, thin black seeds of a water grass native to the Great Lakes region and Mississippi Valley. *See also page 103.*

Wolf-fish: a fish similar in appearance to catfish (and also known as sea catfish) with firm flesh and good flavour. Its prominent sharp teeth can grind up sea urchins, crabs and other shellfish, and because of its alarmingly ferocious looks it is usually sold in fillets or cutlets.

Yam: a starchy tuber of the *Dioscorea* family, rich in vitamin A and similar in taste to the potato. The various types of yam are less sweet and less widely available than sweet potatoes, with which they are sometimes confused—sweet potatoes are often sold as yams in the United States. *See also* Sweet potato.

CONVERSION CHART

These figures are not exact equivalents, but have been rounded up or down slightly to make measuring easier.

Weight Equivalents		Volume Equivalents	
Metric	Imperial	Metric	Imperial
15 g	½ oz	8 cl	3 fl oz
30 g	1 oz	12.5 cl	4 fl oz
60 g	2 oz	15 cl	¼ pint
90 g	3 oz	17.5 cl	6 fl oz
125 g	¼ lb	25 cl	8 fl oz
150 g	5 oz	30 cl	½ pint
200 g	7 oz	35 cl	12 fl oz
250 g	½ lb	45 cl	¾ pint
350 g	¾ lb	50 cl	16 fl oz
500 g	1 lb	60 cl	1 pint
1 kg	2 to 2¼ lb	1 litre	35 fl oz

Cover: What could be more American than a Texan T-bone steak? This one has been seasoned with a marinade of oil, garlic and black pepper, then cooked to perfection over a charcoal barbecue (*recipe, page 112*). The meal is completed with a classic Caesar salad—crunchy cos lettuce mixed with fried bacon and bread cubes, and tossed with Parmesan cheese (*recipe, page 42*)—and a plain baked potato topped with butter. Washed down with an ice-cold American beer, it makes the perfect outdoor feast for a warm summer's day.

TIME-LIFE BOOKS

COOKERY AROUND THE WORLD
English edition staff for *America*
Editorial: Christine Noble (*Editorial Manager*), Felicity Jackson, Ilse Gray, Kate Cann, Mark Stephenson
Designer: Dawn McGinn
Production: Emma Wishart, Justina Cox
Technical Consultant: Michael A. Barnes

English translation by Isabel Varea for Ros Schwartz Translations, London

Published originally under the title *Küchen der Welt: Amerika* by Gräfe und Unzer Verlag GmbH, Munich
© 1995 Gräfe und Unzer Verlag GmbH, Munich

This edition published by Time-Life Books B.V. Amsterdam
Authorized English language edition
© 1995 Time-Life Books B.V.
First English language printing 1995

TIME-LIFE is a trademark of Time Warner Inc. U.S.A.

ISBN 0 7054 3510 5

GRÄFE UND UNZER

Editor: Dr Stephanie von Werz-Kovacs
Sub-Editor: Angela Hermann
Designer: Konstantin Kern
Recipes tested by: Traute Hatterscheid, Barbara Hagman, Dorothea Henghuber, Christa Konrad-Seiter, Doris Leitner
Production: VerlagsService Neuberger & Shaumann GmbH, Heimstetten
Cartography: Huber, Munich
Illustrations: Werner Opitz

Angela G. Grant was born and raised in Washington. She inherited an enthusiasm for American cooking from her mother, and after college she began collecting recipes for fun from all over the United States. She now lives in New York where she has a busy practice as a dietician. This collection of authentic American recipes is her first cookery book.

FoodPhotography Eising Pete A. Eising and Susanne Eising specialize in food and drink photography and work closely with a food photographic agency operating in Germany and Switzerland. As well as cookery publishers, their clients include advertising agencies, industrial companies, newspapers and magazines. The food and props stylist responsible for this volume was Martina Görlach, assisted by Ulla Krause.

Werner Opitz was born in Sprottau (Silesia) in 1942. While serving an apprenticeship as a photoengraver/retoucher, he took drawing lessons with the Essen painter, Fritz Rudert. In 1965 he became a freelance artist. He has painted scenes of the USA since 1983.

Picture Credits

All photographs by FoodPhotography Eising, unless specified below.

Cover: Graham Kirk, London. 4-5, top left (cowboy in Arizona) and top right (truck driver in the Midwest): Paul Spierenburg, Kiel; top centre (Statue of liberty): Gesche M. Cordes, Hamburg; centre (beauty queens in Arizona) and bottom left (native American boy in New Mexico): Rainer Hackenberg, Cologne; bottom right (pavement artist in southern California) and bottom centre (New Orleans musician): Marion Müller, Munich. 8-9 (poster in Los Angeles–Fred Astaire, Humphrey Bogart, Marilyn Monroe): Andreas Gross/J.D., Munich. 10, top: Marton Radkai/J.D., Munich; bottom: Martin Thomas, Munich. 11: Paul Spierenburg, Kiel. 12, top: Erhard Pansegrau, Berlin; bottom: Thomas Stankiewicz, Munich. 13, top: Paul Spierenburg, Kiel; bottom: Erhard Pansegrau, Berlin. 14: Birgit Rademacker, Munich. 15: Barbara Dombrowski/J.D., Munich. 16-17: Thomas Stankiewicz, Munich. 17: Volkmar Janicke/J.D., Munich. 18 (2), 19: Andreas Gross/J.D., Munich. 20: Silvestris Fotoservice, Kastl. 21, top: Rainer Hackenberg, Cologne; bottom: Marion Müller, Munich. 22 (2): Wilfried Becker, Munich. 23: Paul Spierenburg, Kiel. 24: Norbert Hein/J.D., Munich. 25, top: Thomas Stankiewicz, Munich; bottom: Martin Thomas, Munich. 29: Stockfood Eising, Munich. 59: Martin Thomas, Munich. 86: Stockfood Eising, Munich. 111: Andreas Gross/J.D., Munich.

Special thanks to Polo Ralph Lauren for supplying props for the photographs.

Colour reproduction by Fotolito Longo, Bolzano, Italy
Output by A. Creative Text Limited, London, England
Printed and bound by Mondadori, Verona, Italy